# The Book of Pet Love & Loss

### WORDS *of* COMFORT & WISDOM
### *from* REMARKABLE PEOPLE

SARA BADER

SIMON & SCHUSTER

New York | London | Toronto | Sydney | New Delhi

Simon & Schuster
1230 Avenue of the Americas
New York, NY 10020

First Simon & Schuster hardcover edition June 2023

SIMON & SCHUSTER and colophon are registered trademarks of
Simon & Schuster, Inc.

For information about special discounts for bulk purchases, please
contact Simon & Schuster Special Sales at 1-866-506-1949 or
business@simonandschuster.com.

The Simon & Schuster Speakers Bureau can bring authors to your
live event. For more information or to book an event, contact the
Simon & Schuster Speakers Bureau at 1-866-248-3049 or visit our
website at www.simonspeakers.com.

Cover and interior design by Mia Johnson

Manufactured in China

10  9  8  7  6  5  4  3  2  1

Library of Congress Cataloging-in-Publication Data
has been applied for.

ISBN 978-1-9821-3431-0
ISBN 978-1-9821-3433-4 (ebook)

# Contents

## INTRODUCTION

---

In the fall of 2012, I said goodbye to my thirteen-year-old cat, Snowflake. The grief was breathtaking, in a literal sense: it took the wind out of me. I had tried to brace myself, but I've since learned that it's impossible to prepare. In the days and weeks that followed, I couldn't focus and barely ate. I missed her reassuring presence beside me when I fell asleep at night and dreaded waking up to the awful reality that she was no longer here. Snowflake's absence had created, in Steinbeck's words, a "jagged hole" in my life.

Disoriented and overwhelmed, I did what I often do in crisis: I searched for a book that could guide me through that painful time. I knew what I wanted to read: memories, advice, and encouragement from others who had been down the same path—small portions of literary nourishment that would provide solace and perspective without requiring sustained concentration.

I wanted to hear the voices of familiar cultural figures who understood the experience and felt compelled to write or talk about it. I hoped their words might serve as trail markers for me.

I couldn't find this book—in or out of print. I did find a few quotations that were gems, which I saved to reread. Those lines helped carry me through that difficult year—and confirmed what I had sensed early on: that a volume of quotations on pet loss should be out in the world. And so I got to work building the book I wanted to read. I started researching firsthand accounts of pet loss published over the last two centuries. I read journals and biographies, letter collections and memoirs, essays and articles. I listened to oral histories, interviews, and podcasts. I looked out for stories unfolding on social media.

I soon learned that the intensity of my grief for Snowflake was personal and specific, but not unique. Mourners documented their heartache over the loss of their cats, dogs, rabbits, birds, horses, mice, frogs, and other animals—even, in the case of Pablo Neruda, a mongoose. Nobel Prize–winning author V. S. Naipaul described the experience as "calamitous," and writer May Sarton called it a "volcanic eruption of woe." Poet Emily Dickinson was so bereft she asked for help: "Carlo died," she announced in a letter to her friend Thomas Wentworth Higginson in January 1866. "Will you instruct me now?"

Again and again, I came across examples of mourners blindsided and leveled by the loss of a faithful friend.

"Blemie's death was a blow," confessed the playwright Eugene O'Neill to a friend. "I knew I would miss him badly when he went, but I had no idea how badly." Crime novelist Raymond Chandler and his wife were wrecked: "We were a bit broken up over the death of our black Persian cat. When I say a bit broken up I am being conventional. For us it was tragedy." Cat behaviorist Jackson Galaxy offers this visual: "The immediacy of the loss blows through you as if you were an abandoned farmhouse."

How do we make sense of the desolation that sets in so quickly? The bond is unlike any other relationship in our lives. When we're kids, sometimes our dearest friend and closest ally is the family pet. "I can still see my first dog in all the moods and situations that memory has filed him away in . . ." recalled E. B. White. "For six years he met me at the same place after school and convoyed me home—a service he thought up himself." An animal's love is deep, uncomplicated, unconditional, and forgiving, blessedly unburdened by the complexities of human dynamics. "Affection without ambivalence" is how Sigmund Freud described the connection. "No matter how awful the day, or how awful I am behaving at any given moment, George doesn't care," writes the journalist John Dickerson. "He finds me smoldering in my chair and dashes to my lap. Every dog is a rescue dog."

Meanwhile, our daily routines are intricately intertwined. Together, over time, we establish rituals that are as steady as a metronome. And then, at the end, we are often in the position of deciding when to let them go—and if given the privilege, accompanying them in their final moments. It's no wonder that we're devastated when they depart; to be honest, it's a small miracle that we find a way to continue on.

*The Book of Pet Love & Loss* is a guide of sorts. Divided into chapters, the collection walks us down five distinct trails: the celebration of the bond; the realization that the end is near; the adjustment to life without one's shadow; the persistence of mourning; and the final gift of the friendship. Interspersed throughout are photographs of a selection of the cultural figures quoted in the book—with their pets—along with stories of those relationships: Julia Child and her tricolored cat Minette; Billie Holiday and her boxer Mister; Marc Maron and his ginger cat Monkey; Fred Rogers and his childhood dog Mitzi; Beatrix Potter and her mouse Xarifa; Fiona Apple and her pit bull Janet; and many more. It is the first time these individuals and their respective animals have all been brought together in one place, connected through this shared experience. In that sense, this compendium can be considered its own fellowship of pet love and loss, one that spans both geography and time. You will run into familiar voices throughout, but my hope is that this collection will introduce you to a few new ones as well. A complete list of original sources at the back of the book is provided as a map for further exploration.

The spring after Snowflake died, I adopted a one-year-old cat who had been living on the streets of Brooklyn. A rescue organization had found her and named her Pearl. In the early days, I tried out different names on her, including Frances and Marble, but she would only respond to Pearl, an early sign of her clarity and confidence. "Pearl Bader" sounds like the name of a stage actor from the 1930s, which suits her well. She has a flair for drama and a sense of humor. Her larger-than-life personality is, in nearly every way, the opposite of Snowflake's understated disposition. She chews on paperwork, only destroying important documents that are difficult to replace—leases, contracts, that sort of thing. I am convinced she has a genuine appreciation for the absurdity of life.

Pearl turned ten this winter. She has moved into her elder years, which is hard for me to believe but is now confirmed yearly when the vet gives her a senior checkup. She has grown up alongside the research and writing of this manuscript, and it is not lost on me that our time together is finite.

This is the book I once looked for and couldn't find, and it is the book I will turn to again and again. I hope this collection also provides solace for you.

## CHAPTER 1

# A Circle Around Us Both

In a letter in 1863, Emily Dickinson described her Newfoundland, Carlo, as her "shaggy ally," a perfect description that sounds like it could have been written today. Our bond with an animal is often a private affair, but thankfully Dickinson and other brilliant minds were compelled to write about those friendships. Affection and respect shine through. Like a proud parent, Charles Schulz remembered how his childhood dog, Spike, was a language wizard and understood at least fifty words, including "potato," which he would retrieve on command from the basement. P. G. Wodehouse explained how his tenderhearted Pekingese Squeaky intuitively deferred to her elderly sibling, Wonder.

Not all animals are angels, though, and we also hear about maddening habits and domineering personalities. In correspondence with friends, Raymond Chandler documented the antics of his imperious cat, Taki; and John Steinbeck lamented how his setter Toby "made confetti" out of almost half of the original *Of Mice and Men* manuscript, destroying two months of writing. One can't help but wonder about the shredded draft of that now famous novel.

Animals can introduce chaos into our lives, but they are also uniquely capable of calming us down. Billy Collins and William Styron paid homage to the meditative ritual of the "head clearing" daily dog walk, and Doris Lessing described the sacred moment when she set aside "fret" and "urgency" to simply sit and be with her cat, El Magnifico. Perhaps poet Mary Oliver summed it up best: "I think they are companions in a way that people aren't. They'll lie next to you when you're sad. And they remind us that we're animals, too."

# I just got a dog and I think I'm falling in love with him.

ANDY WARHOL

He & I are inseparable companions, and I have vowed him my perpetual society in exchange for his devotion.

ELIZABETH BARRETT BROWNING

The best kind of background noise is a sleeping dog. I think I write better when my dog's asleep next to me. I'm in love with my dog. His name is Walter and he's one year old. When I'm not with him, I need to talk about him constantly.

OTTESSA MOSHFEGH

I could not believe how much happier I was now that I had Merle in my life. Merely by agreeing to feed her and dispose of her waste, I had opened a portal to a pure, white-light joy that cut through all miseries, personal and structural.

SARAH MILLER

My dog has a number of acquaintances of his own species—as do I—but it is abundantly clear to both of us that there is little company in all the world which we enjoy so much as each other's.

DONNA TARTT

As character he
not only had all the
traits I chiefly care
for in humanity
but had them more
abundantly than most
humans.

———

ETHEL SMYTH

Young Fred Rogers and Mitzi, Latrobe, PA,
early 1940s

# FRED ROGERS

From 1968 to 2001, Fred Rogers hosted *Mister Rogers' Neighborhood*, a pioneering children's show that aired on public television. Singing and speaking directly with his audience, Rogers helped raise a nation of young minds through messages of compassion, courage, sharing, and self-love. He believed that children could easily spot inauthenticity, and that "one of the greatest gifts you can give anybody is the gift of your honest self." He also had faith in his viewers: he trusted they could manage complex feelings, and he hoped that what he was offering through words and music could help them process those emotions.

On March 23, 1970, he pulled off something profound on television: he introduced his young audience to the concepts of death and grief. The episode starts off routinely enough. Mister Rogers enters the set singing the theme music and acts out the signature opening scene: he removes his blazer, hangs it in the closet, swaps it for his cardigan, and replaces his dress shoes with more comfortable sneakers. Soon he is standing in front of his aquarium and notices that one of his fish is lying motionless at the bottom of the tank.

Rogers gently removes the goldfish and, after acknowledging that it can't be saved, carefully buries it in the backyard. The experience reminds him of his childhood pet, Mitzi.

"I had a dog that I loved very much . . ." he tells his viewers. "And when she died, I cried, and my grandmother heard me crying, I remember, and she came and she just put her arm around me because she knew I was sad. She knew how much I loved that dog." Back inside, he remembers Mitzi's prickly fur and curly tail. "Would you like to see a picture of her? I think I have one in the drawer here." He dusts off the photo and turns it to the camera.

It was radical to speak so plainly to children about death in televised programming. But Rogers was attuned to his audience and understood what they were ready to hear. In a few minutes of airtime, he explained that death is natural and that sadness is part of the human experience, much like happiness. He showed children how to acknowledge and share their sorrow, a lesson they could carry through life.

When I was little and didn't have a sister yet, my best friend was a brown, wire-haired mongrel named Mitzi. We shared joyous times, exciting times, and sad times. We got scared together when there was thunder and lightning, and together we crawled under the bed until they went away. When I wasn't scared of them any more, Mitzi still was, so I comforted her and felt all the braver.

FRED ROGERS

I didn't have any brothers or sisters, and cats and books were my best friends when I was growing up. I loved to sit on the veranda with a cat, sunning myself.

I can still see my first dog in all the moods and situations that memory has filed him away in.... For six years he met me at the same place after school and convoyed me home—a service he thought up himself. A boy doesn't forget that sort of association.

E. B. WHITE

For companionship I kept pets. I had a cat and a mouse. It's hard to believe that's what I had—it may explain a little of what I am. A little white mouse, Gladys. I would bring her to school and have a chat in the French lesson when it got boring.... Gladys was true and trusted.

KEITH RICHARDS

The walk is the basic unit of the human-and-dog commerce of unconditional love. We take care of George and George takes care of us. No matter how awful the day, or how awful I am behaving at any given moment, George doesn't care. He finds me smoldering in my chair and dashes to my lap. Every dog is a rescue dog.

JOHN DICKERSON

I walk every morning for
a couple of miles with the dog.
That's as much for me as it is
for her; it's head clearing.

BILLY COLLINS

For the last four or five years, whenever
I am home—which has been most
of the time—I have been accustomed to
taking long daily walks with my dog,
Aquinnah. Our walks are for business
and pleasure, and also for survival—
interlocking motives that have
somehow acquired nearly equal
importance in my mind.

WILLIAM STYRON

Julia Child and alert Minette in their Paris
apartment, ca. 1953

# JULIA CHILD

Long before we knew her as the legendary chef and
television personality Julia Child, she was Julia Carolyn
McWilliams, a girl growing up in Pasadena, California,
alongside her siblings and family dog, an energetic
Airedale named Eric the Red. She didn't become a
"cat person" until her mid-thirties, when she and her
husband, Paul Child, moved to Paris in 1948. While
Paul worked in the US Foreign Service, Julia enrolled in
the prestigious Cordon Bleu, where she trained in the
art of French cooking. It was in Paris that she started
testing recipes, collaborating on a cookbook, and, with
her coauthors, teaching informal cooking classes out of
her kitchen.

The Childs rented a drafty apartment on rue de
l'Université that came with a lovely view—and mice.
To keep the rodents at bay, their housekeeper brought
over a cat. Minette was a tricolored wonder: "This pussy
of ours is just a darling," Julia wrote. "I have never seen
a cat I liked so much; she gallops all over the house,
lies in wait for us, sits in her own chair in the dining
room, just loves to be right with us all the time." When
Minette started eating a handpicked bouquet of mimosa
flowers, her name was lengthened to Minette Mimosa
McWilliams Child.

Paul's career uprooted the couple frequently: after France, they moved to Germany, then Norway before settling in Cambridge, Massachusetts. Wherever they lived, neighborhood felines tended to find their way to Julia's kitchens. "A cat—any cat—is necessary to Julia's inner satisfaction," Paul wrote to his brother.

Before Julia established herself as an international culinary sensation—before the publication of the two-volume bible *Mastering the Art of French Cooking*, and before millions would watch her television show, falling in love with her enthusiasm, humor, and unpretentious approach to gourmet cooking—Minette, perched on a shelf above the stove, occupied the front-row seat in one of history's finest test kitchens.

"Mini" soon became an important part of our lives.... She spent a great deal of time playing with a Brussels sprout tied to a string, or peering under our radiators with her tail switching. Once in a while, she'd proudly present us with a mouse. She was my first cat ever, and I thought she was marvelous.

JULIA CHILD

This you'll call
sentimental—
perhaps—but then
a dog somehow
represents—no I can't
think of the word—the
private side of life—
the play side.

---

VIRGINIA WOOLF

My rabbit is a big part of my life, and I like to include her at all my get-togethers. . . . In fact, my apartment is completely designed around my rabbit. I have chosen paint colors based on their names alone: straw, dandelion green, carrot orange, leaf grass, marsh brown. My couch is covered with a cloverleaf print. My liquor cabinet was built to resemble a small tree so that my apartment has a woodsy feel to it.

———

AMY SEDARIS

At home where we live in Corona is *so lively*. We have *two* dogs. They are *Schnauzers*, Male + Female.... The Male Dog who is the older one, his name is "Trumpet." The Female, the baby, her name is "Trinket." I gave Trumpet to Lucille and Mr. Joe Glaser gave us Trinket. And when the two of them start barking together—*Oh Boy* what a *Duet*.

LOUIS ARMSTRONG

I don't sing to Tamas, but I do
sometimes dance, which terrifies him—
he runs from place to place as though
for shelter and barks his dismay.
I must seem to him like some terrifying
goddess on a rampage.

MAY SARTON

I love to house my little people happily—
my dogs and my birds and my fish.
Wee Toi, my little Chinese dog, has a
little house all his own, an old Chinese
lacquer box with a canopy top and little
gold bells. . . . Wee Toi is very happy in
it, and you can see that it was meant for
him in the beginning.

ELSIE DE WOLFE

Liberace surrounded by his dogs on his patio,
Palm Springs, CA, 1980

# LIBERACE

"I didn't come here to go unnoticed," Liberace told the *London Evening News* when he arrived at the Palladium in a white mink coat in 1972. Władziu Valentino Liberace ("Lee" to his friends; "Walter" or "Wally" to his family) was born on May 16, 1919, in West Allis, Wisconsin. He began learning piano when he was four years old, and by the time he was a teenager, he was playing professionally. Over his long career, the mononymous performing artist and highest-paid entertainer of the 1960s perfected his over-the-top showmanship.

Liberace subscribed to Mae West's maxim "Too much of a good thing can be wonderful." He applied that philosophy to his stage act, opulent homes, wardrobe, jewelry, and animals. "I have a lot of dogs," he admitted. "The number changes all the time. So if I ever happen to mention a dog's name and it is not the same name I mentioned the last time I mentioned a dog's name, it's not a mistake. It's another dog." He chose playful names with as much flair as his act, including Wrinkles and Prunella for his shar-peis; Lady and the Tramp for his Yorkshire terriers; Jacques, Michi, and Bonaparte for his three poodles; Lady Di for his West Highland terrier; and Liza for the Welsh corgi who was a direct descendant of one of Queen Elizabeth's dogs.

Many were rescues, given to him by someone who could no longer care for the animal. They had full run of his lavish homes: "They are allowed anywhere," he explained, "and they respect my rugs and furniture better than some people I've entertained."

By 1976, he counted fourteen canines in his care; ten years later, that number had multiplied: "If somebody were to ask me why a single man needs so many homes, I could reply it's because I have so many children. Twenty-one, to be exact . . ." he wrote in his memoir. "I'd better explain that my 'children' are my dogs. And I couldn't love them more if I'd sired the whole litter." On tour, he missed his animals tremendously. "When I travel, I carry framed pictures of them to place around the hotel suites. . . . I call home long distance just to speak to them. When they hear the sound of my voice on the phone, they literally go 'crazy.'"

When Liberace died at sixty-seven, he left $50,000 in his will for the care of his beloved dogs.

I have one dog, Lady Di, who will try to "sing" whenever I play the piano. The real singer in the family is Julio, a canary who sings up a storm every time I put on one of Julio Iglesias's records.

LIBERACE

The dachshunds have been running through all the rooms, being affectionate, barking at the servants. They were fed and then they began to feel utterly at home. At night they dug the earth and newly-sown seed from the window boxes and distributed the galoshes from the lobby round all the rooms. . . . But both have kind, grateful eyes.

ANTON CHEKHOV

Our cat is growing positively tyrannical. If she finds herself alone anywhere she emits blood-curdling yells until somebody comes running. She sleeps on a table in the service porch and now demands to be lifted up and down from it. She gets warm milk about eight o'clock at night and starts yelling for it about 7:30. When she gets it she drinks a little, goes off and sits under a chair, then comes and yells all over again for someone to stand beside her while she has another go at the milk.

RAYMOND CHANDLER

It is amusing to see the kitty act like a dog.... Yesterday, the cat, seeing that I compliment Spot for bringing me the paper, went across the street and got a small piece of paper and brought it to me, too. I praised her and petted her, and she was as proud as punch.

———

ZORA NEALE HURSTON

I don't know whether
I told you. My setter pup,
left alone one night, made
confetti of about half
of my manuscript. Two
months work to do over
again. It sets me back.
There was no other draft.
I was pretty mad but the
poor little fellow may have
been acting critically.

JOHN STEINBECK

# CHARLES SCHULZ

The illustrator behind the heartfelt comic strip *Peanuts* created what has been described as "arguably the longest story ever told by one human being." In nearly eighteen thousand strips published for almost fifty years in seventy-five countries and twenty-one languages, Charles Schulz convinced a universe of readers to care about Charlie Brown, Linus, Lucy, Peppermint Patty, Snoopy, Woodstock, and their crew of friends. These "little people," as Schulz called them, were not cartoon outlines; he conjured complex characters with their own worries, insecurities, and preferences. (Snoopy hung a Vincent van Gogh painting in his doghouse, which he later swapped for a work by Andrew Wyeth.)

Schulz loved dogs throughout his life, but one in particular inspired the character of Snoopy. When Schulz was thirteen years old, his family brought home a black-and-white mutt they named Spike. Exceptionally bright, Spike taught himself to ring the back doorbell when he wanted to come inside. Amused by the inquisitive personality of the floppy-eared dog, Schulz submitted a one-panel cartoon of Spike to *Ripley's Believe It or Not*. It was published on February 22, 1937, along with the caption: "A hunting dog that eats pins, tacks, and razor blades is owned by C. F. Schulz, St. Paul, Minn." This was an early image of what would become Snoopy, the beagle who shared Spike's markings. (Schulz saved the name "Spike" for Snoopy's mustached brother, who lives on his own in the California desert.)

Schulz's childhood dog made a lasting impression on the cartoonist, but he shared the deepest bond with another dog later in his life. In 1988, Schulz and his wife adopted a scruffy eight-year-old fox terrier with the name "Andy" scratched on the inside of his leather collar. Giving Andy a comfortable life was Schulz's priority. "Well, I am going home now," he would announce to his colleagues as he left the studio in the late afternoon. "I'm going to devote the rest of the day to making my dog happy."

When Andy's vision and hearing began to deteriorate, the couple nailed a sign to a tree in the driveway of their Santa Rosa, California, house: "Please drive slowly. Small dog does not see or hear well." And when Andy died, the cartoonist shared his heartache with his readers: "He had been an unbelievable joy to me, and as I write this I am deeply sorrowful. . . . Andy brought some new truths into my life. He taught me the wonderful love that a person can have for a dog."

His love for Andy also made its way into a *Peanuts* strip. Charlie Brown and Linus gaze at a night sky full of stars as Linus contemplates the mysteries of the universe and the hundred billion galaxies out there, each containing a hundred billion stars. "Sort of puts things in perspective, doesn't it?" Linus asks.

"I miss my dog," replies Charlie Brown.

Snoopy's not a real dog, of course—he's an image of what people would like a dog to be. But he has his origins in Spike, my dog that I had when I was a kid. White with black spots. He was the wildest and smartest dog I've ever encountered. Smart? Why, he had a vocabulary of at least fifty words. I mean it. I'd tell him to go down to the basement and bring up a potato and he'd do it.

CHARLES SCHULZ

My dog and my mongoose were my sole companions. Fresh from the jungle, the latter grew up at my side, slept in my bed, and ate at my table. No one can imagine the affectionate nature of a mongoose. My little pet was familiar with every minute of my day-to-day life, she tramped all over my papers, and raced after me all day long. She curled up between my shoulder and my head at siesta time and slept there the fitful, electric sleep of wild animals.

PABLO NERUDA

I used to carry the green parrot around on my shoulder. I carried him all over the Sahara. They're very good to travel with.

They're happy, they're not miserable traveling. You try to travel with a cat, and it's miserable. Parrots don't mind moving. They really attach themselves to a person, and the place they're in be damned.

PAUL BOWLES

There was one pigeon, a beautiful bird, pure white with light gray tips on its wings; that one was different. It was a female. I would know that pigeon anywhere. No matter where I was, that pigeon would find me; when I wanted her I had only to wish and call her and she would come flying to me. She understood me and I understood her. I loved that pigeon.

NIKOLA TESLA

I tell my dog my troubles. I tell my dog what I'm not supposed to be saying to my children, to my wife. Unfortunately, it's not very helpful to her because she has to hear it, but at least the world doesn't hear my inner thoughts.

MANDY PATINKIN

I've got two cats, Spikey and Silver, and they're my personality chopped in half. One of them is really outgoing, loves me and loves visitors, and the other goes, "Oh my God, not another person, please!" That's totally me in the cats.

JEANETTE WINTERSON

Robert Frost and Gillie, Ripton, VT

# ROBERT FROST

Robert Frost is an American icon, the recipient of four Pulitzers, and the first poet to read at a presidential inauguration—John F. Kennedy's in 1961. With plain-spoken words, he hoped to create a lasting body of work and "to lodge a few poems where they will be hard to get rid of," goals he far surpassed. "The Road Not Taken" is perhaps the most widely recognized poem of the twentieth century. He was also an esteemed educator and credits that role for teaching him how to write clearly: "I had to make things understood, and that put me in the class of poets that wanted to be understood."

New England was Frost's home and the subject of much of his poetry. For most of his career, he split his time between college towns and farms in New Hampshire, then Vermont—ideal settings for a dog. In 1940, Frost opened his heart to a border collie named Gillie, an extraordinary gift, it turned out, for both of them. "His virtues are all gentle," Frost described in a letter to his son-in-law.

Frost's wife, Elinor, had died two years earlier, and Gillie helped fill the void. Together they explored the woods surrounding his cabin in Vermont and walked the streets near his home in Cambridge, Massachusetts. Frost often wrote late into the night—he did his best work between midnight and 4 a.m.—and he and Gillie could be seen taking predawn strolls through the neighborhood.

Gillie was intelligent and eager to please—a "one-man dog," recalled a neighbor who lived a few doors down from the poet in Cambridge: "Sometimes Mr. Frost, while in the midst of a conversation with someone, would say without raising his voice, 'Gillie, shut the door, will you?' and Gillie would get up, go to the door, push it shut and then stand, watching his master's face and waiting for further orders."

The poet David McCord, who visited the Frost home often—the two writers would talk for hours in the library—also observed the understanding that Frost and his border collie shared: "When at last we went out for a walk—a ritual on the poet's part and always best under stars, Gillie was there, not a yard behind his master's leg," McCord recalled. He would let Gillie explore the darkness off leash, while gently keeping him safe and near. "Frost would say quietly—no whistle or calling—'You better come back, Gillie,' or something like that; and out of the dark as out of the mystery of life itself, a shadow would slip to heel."

I have a black dog with white nose tip, white tail tip, white shirt and white stockings.... He's very intelligent and watches everything I do in hope that it will mean food or play or a walk for him. He's no fighter though. He's a pacifist.

ROBERT FROST

Whenever it is possible, my dog accompanies me on a walk or ride or sail. I have had many dog friends—huge mastiffs, soft-eyed spaniels, wood-wise setters and honest, homely bull terriers. At present the lord of my affections is one of these bull terriers.... My dog friends seem to understand my limitations, and always keep close beside me when I am alone. I love their affectionate ways and the eloquent wag of their tails.

HELEN KELLER

I talk of all these things with Carlo, and his eyes grow meaning, and his shaggy feet keep a slower pace.

EMILY DICKINSON

When I sit down to be with him, it means slowing myself down, getting rid of the fret and the urgency. When I do this—and he must be in the right mood too, not in pain or restless—then he subtly lets me know he understands I am trying to reach him, reach cat, essence of cat, finding the best of him. Human and cat, we try to transcend what separates us.

DORIS LESSING

Pekes.
How understanding
they are. When Squeaky
is on my lap and sees that
Wonder wants to get on,
she instantly jumps off,
as she knows that W. is
the senior dog and nearly
fifteen and must be
put first. But then Squeaky
is an angel from heaven.

P. G. WODEHOUSE

He was as solid a trail horse as I've ever ridden, never flinching in big wind, or while crossing water, or when mule deer twins who'd been stashed by their mother in some willows leaped to their feet right in front of him.... I counted on Roany to keep the whole barnyard calm, not just Deseo and the mini donkeys, but also the ewes and lambs, the recalcitrant rams, the aging chickens, and me.

PAM HOUSTON

# BILLIE HOLIDAY

In June 1946, Billie Holiday sang at Club Downbeat on 52nd Street in New York City. Music journalist and photographer William Gottlieb captured Holiday backstage in the dressing room with her dog Mister. The dignified, gentle boxer sits on a chair next to the singer, looking at the camera. Holiday is wearing her signature gardenias in her hair; her right hand rests on the dog's chest. Objects reflected in the dressing room's mirror reveal her rituals: face powder, pineapple to soothe her throat, bottle of crème de menthe. It is an intimate and serene portrait of the jazz legend, whose life was cut short by addiction.

When Gottlieb snapped this photograph, Holiday was already one of the most celebrated jazz vocalists of all time. She started singing in Harlem nightclubs in the early 1930s, when she was a teenager, and collaborating with musicians—Benny Goodman, Count Basie, Artie Shaw, Lester Young—as the Harlem Renaissance was transitioning to the swing era. She first performed her rendition of the protest song "Strange Fruit" at the Café Society club in 1939, engraving the devastating lyrics into our collective memory.

Lady Day, the name Young coined for her, died when she was just forty-four. In portraits of the legend in casual settings, one of her beloved dogs is often in the frame—especially Mister in the 1940s and Chiquita or Pepe, two Chihuahuas, in the 1950s. Mister, in particular, holds a special place in music history. He and Holiday were inseparable. He patiently waited backstage or sometimes in the bar while she sang. "As long as he heard her voice, he's happy," recalled the vaudevillian comedian Harold Cromer, who often performed in the same venues.

In 1949, when the photographer Herman Leonard visited Holiday's Harlem apartment for an *Ebony* magazine photo shoot, she opened the door wearing an apron over her dress. "Excuse me," she told him, "but I've got to feed the dog." A photograph from the day fills in details: the jazz singer at the stove frying a steak in a cast-iron skillet for Mister, who sits beside her. Mister's steady disposition must have grounded Holiday. "The thing I remember talking to her about most were her dogs," Lena Horne recalled. "Her animals were really her only trusted friends."

*overleaf*: Billie Holiday and Mister in her dressing room at Club Downbeat, New York City, ca. 1946

I knew Mister wouldn't
recognize me. . . . I had gained
so much weight and I just plain
didn't look like the girl who had
left town ten months before. . . .
Man, how cheap I played that dog!
He not only recognized me,
but in a flash he leaped at me,
kicked my hat off, and knocked
me flat on my can in the middle of
that little station. Then he began
lapping me and loving
me like crazy.

BILLIE HOLIDAY

Tulip never let me down. She is nothing if not consistent. She knows where to draw the line, and it is always in the same place, a circle around us both.

J. R. ACKERLEY

The dog and I have a walk almost every early morning and again at sunset—He just now banged on the door to tell me he was ready to come in and go to bed.

GEORGIA O'KEEFFE

When it is bedtime I pick her up, cuddle her, whisper what a sweet creature she is, how beautiful and wonderful, how lucky I am to have her in my life, and that I will love her always. I take her to her room, with its cat door for her après-midnight exitings, and gently place her on her bed. In the morning when I wake up she is already outside, quietly sitting on the railing, eyes closed, meditating.

ALICE WALKER

Purring in his sleep,
Fletch stretches out
his little black paws
to touch my hands,
the claws withdrawn,
just a gentle touch to
assure him that I am
there beside him
as he sleeps.

WILLIAM S. BURROUGHS

I really like it
when he sleeps
at the top of
my head on the
pillow like a sort
of fur nightcap.

———

URSULA K. LE GUIN

My relationship with my two old cats Monkey and LaFonda is the longest I've ever had. We all understand each other and show up for each other in the ways we can and it's good.

MARC MARON

I can't imagine my life without my cat. It's as though it doesn't make sense. If someone asked me to truly describe myself in an abstract frame, next to me there would be a small mark, like a smudge, and that small mark would be my cat.

TRACEY EMIN

# EDWARD GOREY

"What or who is the greatest love of your life?" *Vanity Fair* asked the legendary author and artist Edward Gorey in 1997.

"Cats," he replied.

For almost fifty years, felines kept Gorey company while he wrote and illustrated more than one hundred books. Gorey's delicate pen-and-ink drawings, precise hand-lettered text, and dark plots continue to enchant readers of all ages. Although his Victorian and Edwardian characters often endure grim fates, his deadpan humor brilliantly offsets the gloom and doom.

Gorey, who died in 2000, was often described as reclusive, although his physical presence—six feet two, long beard—was hard to miss: "I'm not someone easily unnoticed," he told an interviewer in 1973. "I've always tended to run around in tennis shoes, fur coats, lots of jewelry. I just can't go out of the house with naked fingers."

When he was seven years old he got his first cat, and aside from his years in the army and as an undergraduate at Harvard, he lived with a revolving cast of felines. He couldn't imagine a life without them. He moved to New York City in 1953 to work as a cover designer at Anchor Books, and shared his rent-controlled apartment with as many as a half dozen cats. He noticed a tipping point once the number hit six: "Between four and five didn't seem much difference. . . . But somehow six cats seem a lot more, disproportionately more, than five."

Eventually he left his staff job to work as a freelancer and continued to conjure his magical, melancholy worlds in print. He also designed the costumes and sets for a 1977 Broadway production of *Dracula*, a huge hit. For decades he split his time between New York City and Cape Cod. (Each year, Gorey attended nearly every New York City Ballet performance and decamped for the ocean once the season ended.)

In 1986 he left Manhattan for good and settled in a sea captain's home in Yarmouth Port, Massachusetts. He lived in that book-filled two-hundred-year-old house with his feline family. They lounged on him and his drawing board while he worked, and if one of his cats accidentally knocked over a bottle of india ink, spilling black liquid over a drawing he had been tirelessly crosshatching, Gorey accepted the chaos with calm resignation. "Most people who have cats would not put up with what I put up with from my cats," he admitted. "But I feel it's their house as much as mine. . . . It's very interesting sharing a house with a group of people who obviously see things, hear things, think about things in a vastly different way."

His house—their house—is now a museum. He left his estate to a charitable trust that helps protect cats as well as dogs, whales, elephants, birds, bats, insects, and invertebrates.

In looking for something or other I came across the fact that one of my cats is about to be nine years old, and that another of them will shortly thereafter be eight; I have been laboring under the delusion they were about five or six.

EDWARD GOREY

# My little old dog:
# A heart-beat
# At my feet.

EDITH WHARTON

Dogs have such short life spans, it's like
a concentrated version of a human life. When
they get older they become much more like our
mothers. They wait for us, watch out for us, are
completely fascinated by everything we do.
So, with [Lucille], she's the kid I never got to be
and the mother I never quite had. It's really quite
remarkable how much they can provide without
any prompting. It's just built into the species.

CAROLINE KNAPP


My beloved Chihuahua Pepsi is never far from
me, night or day: she is now over ten years old and
spends 90% of her time sleeping—but is always
ready to pick a fight with Minnie, our Yorkshire
terrier. After a succession of sadly missed
shepherds and ridgebacks, I never imagined I
would lose my heart to so tiny a canine person.

ARTHUR C. CLARKE

It is nearly dark outside and the roof is cold. My cat will be making her way along the sycamore limb and I must be there waiting to lift her to my shoulder. Today I found fresh swordfish in the market, and she has never tasted swordfish. Maybe she'll be tempted.

IRVING TOWNSEND

## CHAPTER 2

# Their Time Must Come

The first signs that they are slowing down are often so subtle, we barely notice. They nap more. They hesitate before stairs. They walk gingerly over rough gravel roads and are less inclined to take off in a joyful sprint. Their muzzle starts to show a bit of white frost. And yet it also seems to happen overnight: suddenly we realize our companion is getting on in years.

Animals teach us how to live, but they also teach us how to age—how to hold on to optimism and humor, in spite of growing limitations. In a tender tribute to her horse Roany, writer Pam Houston remembers how even when his condition worsened, he still blew bubbles in his water bucket to amuse her.

If we're fortunate enough to accompany an animal through the journey of aging, we're also granted the enormous responsibility of deciding when it's time to say goodbye. It's understandable that we might become overwhelmed by anticipatory grief and focused on how our world will soon change, but the musician Fiona Apple encourages us to try to be present for this final chapter, to "appreciate the time that lies right beside the end of time."

He has filled the
corners of
the room and
the minutes and
me so sweetly
these last years.

---

ALICE B. TOKLAS

A dog lives only ten or fifteen years, but think how much he crowds into that space, how much energy and vitality he lives up.

JOHN BURROUGHS

Oh dear, how old she is, and how touching in her old age, carefully choosing the smoothest bits of road to cross by because gravel and roughness hurt her old paws and make her stumble as she totters along.

———

J. R. ACKERLEY

She's eleven. That's a far cry from eight for a dog, really, and there are mornings these days when she wants to sleep in, and afternoons when she wants to sleep in, and she has started eyeing stairs with reluctance. On occasion, she's creaky and slow to unhinge her hips when she gets up.

———

SUSAN ORLEAN

The greatest problem with Irish Wolfhounds … is that they don't live very long; their great hearts give out. A good deal of this is genetic, of course, but I think it is in part that they worry so for us, care so much.

EDWARD ALBEE

Mary Oliver and Percy at home,
Provincetown, MA, 2005

# MARY OLIVER

The beloved Pulitzer Prize—winning poet Mary Oliver fixed her attention on the natural world. Her life-affirming poetry is dedicated to the art of observation. She encouraged her readers to remain curious about the wonders around them, a sacred duty she carried out daily. Her poems are meditations, often first scribbled down as notes while walking in the woods or along shorelines with her dogs. "I was a bride," she wrote in one poem, "married to amazement." For over fifty years, she translated that amazement into language and imagery that resonates with a wide readership. On the literary landscape, this makes her a rare breed: a bestselling author of poetry.

Along with her partner, photographer Molly Malone Cook, with whom she lived for decades in Provincetown, Massachusetts, Oliver spent much of her time in the company of dogs. She forged meaningful relationships with animals early in her life. Tippy—a dog with a tail tipped in white—was the first: "She was a puppy who showed up at my great-aunt's door, and she made a gift of her to me." In 2013, Oliver published *Dog Songs*, a collection of poems about some of the dogs she had loved through the years—Bear, Luke, Ben, Sammy, Bazougey, Percy, Ricky. Each poem reads like a prayer. She revered her dogs and paid close attention to their habits and movements:

Bear's joy as he gallops through fresh snow; Luke's resilience, a dreamer born in a junkyard; Sammy's irrepressible spirit and urge to jump fences—not to make trouble but to say hello to the neighbors.

Oliver also understood that dogs do not belong to us—they belong to the natural world. "They are a kind of poetry themselves when they are devoted not only to us but to the wet night, to the moon and the rabbit-smell in the grass and their own bodies leaping forward." They grace us with their presence while they are here, and losing them is, in her words, the "deepest sting."

Nature and dogs gave her life shape and meaning. "What would the world be like without music or rivers or the green and tender grass?" she asked. "What would this world be like without dogs?" Unfathomable. For Oliver, a dog running free remained one of the most magnificent sights in the world.

It is exceedingly short, his galloping life. Dogs die so soon. I have my stories of that grief, no doubt many of you do also. It is almost a failure of will, a failure of love, to let them grow old—or so it feels. We would do anything to keep them with us, and to keep them young. The one gift we cannot give.

———

MARY OLIVER

Charley is well but he is getting old.
The hip he had broken as a pup gives him
considerable trouble now, particularly
when the weather changes. But in the
morning he still thinks of himself as Youth.

JOHN STEINBECK

Having an old dog and watching her have
the grace to just slow down and spend
more time in the sun, it was an experience
I would never have wanted to miss. It was,
in many ways, a way that we learned about
death and how to get old, and how to do it,
and how to be there and not just pretend
it wasn't happening.

LAURIE ANDERSON

Tavi, my cocker spaniel, lies at the foot of the bed. He is fourteen years old, the equivalent of eighty years in a man. He is deaf. He does not see very well. He sleeps most of the day. I once thought we would grow old together.

ANAÏS NIN

He is not doing badly, this old cat, with his three legs, and people coming into the room stop and exclaim, What a magnificent cat!—but when he gets up and hobbles away they are silent, particularly if they have seen him as a young cat step proudly out of a room.

DORIS LESSING

Last week, watching Darcy out in the sun, it felt as though I was trying to decide just when most of the life—the good life, that is—inside her has been used up. Is it conscionable to wait until it's plainly gone? Or is it better to err on the side of saying goodbye while she's still discernibly Darcy, while she seems, as she nearly always does, to be without pain?

———

VERLYN KLINKENBORG

When you have dogs, you witness their uncomplaining acceptance of suffering, their bright desire to make the most of life in spite of the limitations of age and disease, their calm awareness of the approaching end when their final hours come. They accept death with a grace that I hope I will one day be brave enough to muster.

DEAN KOONTZ

Tracey Emin and Docket at home, London, 2017

# TRACEY EMIN

Contemporary British artist Tracey Emin set the media world ablaze in 1999 when her controversial installation *My Bed* was shortlisted for the Turner Prize and shown at the Tate Gallery. The story goes like this: After a breakup in 1998, Emin spent several days in bed in a haze of depression. When she emerged, she looked at the rumpled, dirty sheets and messy stash of empty vodka bottles, cigarette packages and butts, and other detritus and decided not to sanitize the scene. Instead she saw an artwork before her: "I just saw it in a white space, I saw it out of that environment and, subconsciously, I saw myself out of that environment, and I saw a way for my future that wasn't a failure, that wasn't desperate." In 2000 Charles Saatchi bought the piece for £150,000 and in 2014 it sold for £2.5 million.

Emin explores themes of love, loss, vulnerability, desire, and grief in confessional installations like *My Bed* but also in drawings, paintings, photography, sculpture, film, neon, embroidery, and ceramics. Given the intimacy of her subject matter, it makes sense that she also explored her bond with Docket, her cat, in her artwork. "Docket is not just a pet to me," she wrote. "Without sounding too corny, he is really like my baby. I constantly say this. I love him more than anything else in the world."

In 2002, Docket disappeared, and Emin blanketed her East London neighborhood with lost-cat flyers. Passersby assumed they were original works of art and unhelpfully removed the posters. "It's simply a notice of her missing cat to alert neighbors," a spokesperson at her gallery clarified. "It's not a conceptual piece of work and it has nothing to do with her art." Docket had wandered into an abandoned house and was soon found. By then, news of the ordeal had traveled in the press and established Docket as one of Britain's most celebrated cats.

Emin and Docket were a unit, their routines intertwined. "My house is five floors; the kitchen is in the basement, and my bedroom is at the top, so I always make a flask of green tea to take to bed with me," she explained in 2013. "On the nights I stay in, I shower, make my tea, and have a cup of Horlicks (warm malted milk) with my cat." Docket died in 2020, at the dignified age of nineteen and a half.

If I'm honest, I realize that I plan a lot of my life around my cat. And by this, I don't mean small things, I mean where I live, who I live with and my future plans. Should I move to the country? Should I live by the sea? Every large-scale decision that I make involves Docket. The idea that he is seriously ill is making me feel confused and afraid.

---

TRACEY EMIN

Roany was stoicism defined. As his condition worsened, he learned to pivot on his good front leg—and would, for an apple or a carrot or to sneak into the barn to get at the winter's stash of alfalfa. He blew bubbles in his water bucket because it made me laugh, and he would sometimes even give himself a birdbath by splashing his still mighty head. I also knew that just because he *could* handle the discomfort didn't mean he *should*.

PAM HOUSTON

What is so touching about a sick animal is the patience and lack of self-pity, and of course the total dependence on human care.

———————

MAY SARTON

# FIONA APPLE

In the spring of 2020, the musician Fiona Apple released her fifth studio album, *Fetch the Bolt Cutters*, which she recorded in her home in Venice, California, with a small band of trusted musicians. The music is visceral. There is chanting and banging on makeshift percussive surfaces, and in one song Apple taps on the urn that holds the ashes of her departed pit bull, Janet. On the titular track, you can hear the sound of dogs barking in the background.

Apple emerged on the music scene in the 1990s. When the producer Andrew Slater first met her, she was a teenager who had been writing songs since she was eight but had never recorded with other musicians. She released her wildly successful debut album, *Tidal*, in 1996, and in less than two years' time, Apple shot from anonymity to the cover of *Rolling Stone*.

It was not a forgiving journey. Critics ridiculed her radical honesty and resistance to the music industry's script for her. She found herself misunderstood, and setting the record straight became an exhausting exercise. She retreated but continued to create music on her own terms and timeline.

When Apple was twenty-one and navigating those early turbulent years in Los Angeles, she found a four-month-old puppy abandoned in a park with a rope tied around her neck and bite marks on her face and ears. The gentle pit bull had been used and then abandoned by dogfighters. Apple named the puppy Janet and the two became family. "She is my best friend, and my mother and my daughter, my benefactor," wrote Apple, "and she's the one who taught me what love is."

In 2012, Apple released her fourth album, *The Idler Wheel. . . .* By then, Janet was elderly and unable to travel. When Apple returned from her US tour, Janet's health had deteriorated, and the musician canceled her South American shows to care for her. In a four-page letter to her fans, handwritten and posted on Facebook, she explained her decision: "These are the choices we make, which define us," she wrote in a stunning articulation of love and devotion. "I will not be the woman who puts her career above love and friendship. I am the woman who stays home, baking Tilapia for my dearest, oldest friend. And helps her be comfortable + comforted + safe + important." She asked her fans for their understanding and blessing. "I'll be seeing you," she signed off. "Love, Fiona."

*overleaf*: Fiona Apple and Janet,
Los Angeles, CA, 2007

Many of us these days, we dread
the death of a loved one. It is
the ugly truth of Life that keeps
us terrified + alone. I wish we
could appreciate the time that
lies right beside the end of time.
I know that I will feel the most
overwhelming knowledge of her,
and of her life and of my love for
her, in the last moments.
I need to do my damnedest,
to be there for that.

———————

FIONA APPLE

I have always loved dogs.
The saddest thing about it is that
they don't live as long as people do.
They come into your life, you love
them, and then they have to go.

DOLLY PARTON

He is enjoying his old age—unconscious of
any of its disadvantages and as you know
a gentle companion. It is an idle hope that
we will jog on together—the catastrophic
proof of the futility of such dreams has
been offered and gradually accepted.

ALICE B. TOKLAS

Anyone who has ever been in a similar position to mine, and who has seen his or her animal carry on a difficult fight, can only love and respect that animal more, particularly when you realize that it takes a very special kind of courage. It takes a courage which is very different from human courage but is, if anything, more worthy of admiration, because human courage comes at least armed with some knowledge, whereas animal courage often comes with no knowledge at all—not even, in the case of disease, knowledge of what it is they fight.

CLEVELAND AMORY

Do they know, as we do, that their time must come? Yes, they know, at rare moments. No other way can I interpret those pauses of his latter life, when, propped on his forefeet, he would sit for long minutes quite motionless—his head drooped, utterly withdrawn; then turn those eyes of his and look at me. That look said more plainly than all words could: "Yes, I know that I must go!"

JOHN GALSWORTHY

Once again a member of my family whose first days I remember well is living out her last beside me.

IRVING TOWNSEND

Do you know that
I believe that the first
to come and greet
me when I go to
heaven will be this
dear, faithful old
friend Carlo?

———

EMILY DICKINSON

Staunch & faithful little
lovers that they are,
they give back a hundred
fold every sign of love
one ever gives them—
& it mitigates the pang
of losing them to know
how very happy a little
affection has made them.

EDITH WHARTON

Studio portrait of Ethel Smyth and Marco,
ca. 1891–94

# ETHEL SMYTH

On March 11, 1903, the Metropolitan Opera in New York City presented the work of a female composer for the first time. That night *Der Wald* (The Forest) by British composer Ethel Smyth was performed on a double bill with Verdi's *Il Trovatore*. (It would take until 2016—one hundred thirteen more years—for the Met to present the work of another female composer.) Although Smyth's opera was a box office success, reviewers were ruthless. The *New York Times* called it a "disappointing novelty" with music that "falls into an inextricable slough of dreariness," and a critic for the *New York World* described *Der Wald* as "utterly unfeminine," lacking in "sweetness and grace of phrase."

Smyth was undeterred. She had already faced years of sexism, starting with her father, who opposed her decision to pursue music composition. She was close with Emmeline Pankhurst, the leader of the British suffrage movement, and Smyth wrote the movement's anthem, "The March of the Women." "I want women to turn their minds to big and difficult jobs, not just to go on hugging the shore," she explained in one of her many memoirs. Outspoken and confident, she was open about her romantic interest in both men and women, including, later in life, her love for Virginia Woolf, twenty-four years her junior.

Smyth preferred to wear tailored tweed suits. She also favored large dogs. Marco was the first, "a huge sprawling yellow-and-white puppy of the long-haired kind." Regarding his breed, the details are hazy: "Half St. Bernard, and the rest what you please." He was succeeded by an Old English sheepdog, whom she named Pan. Over time, there would be Pan the Second, the Third, and the Fourth. The last was her favorite.

Pan the Fourth was eccentric, with a perplexing fondness for white bread. He understood English—not only commands but also sentences, so much so that toward the end of his life, when he was sick, Smyth avoided discussing details of his illness in front of him. His extreme beauty captivated her: "The rich color, quantity, and fabric of his coat, the nobility of his head, and above all the big melting brown eyes that were in a certain light of an almost unearthly quality—so deep, so calm, so steady, so loving were they."

Encouraged by Tchaikovsky when she studied in Germany early on, Smyth would go on to write six operas as well as orchestral works, a ballet, a mass, and more. In 1922, she was appointed a Dame Commander of the Order of the British Empire, the first female composer to hold that title. Her large dogs, who sit next to her or lean on her lap in elegant portraits, supported her throughout: "While I have been writing Marco lies slumbering peacefully at my feet, little knowing what a definite part he has played in my career."

He was sixteen years old, a great age for a big dog, when I felt that the hour for parting had struck at last.

ETHEL SMYTH

Gizmo was a somber cat.
He parked himself on my wife's
chest Friday night and she spoke
to him and scritched him for
a long time. He stood, swaying
slightly. I was smart enough to say
nothing. But my wife had been
talking more and more about not
wanting him to suffer. During
the last fluid infusion, the vet said
something very helpful to us:
"You might want to say goodbye
to him on a good day."

NEIL STEINBERG

My favorite monk at the ashram where I lived in India taught me that dogs have such a short lifespan because it's part of their loving service to us. They are here, among other reasons, to teach us how to die—because they are so good at it, and we are so bad at it. . . . Wanting to help, they volunteer to die early, as a way of saying: "Look! It's not hard! Let me show you how! All you have to do is let go."

ELIZABETH GILBERT

## CHAPTER 3

# It's Tough to Lose Your Shadow

Even when we try to prepare for the loss, the depth of grief can be overwhelming. For nineteenth-century naturalist John Burroughs, the death of his dog Nip stunned him: "It was one of the worst shocks I ever had," he recorded in his journal. "For a moment the whole universe seemed bereft, and my whole outlook upon life changed."

In their absence, our days are reshaped overnight, our shared rituals become irrelevant. Journalist Natalie Angier describes it as "a sorrow of details, of minor rhythms and assumptions that I hadn't really been aware of until, suddenly, they were disrupted or unmet." Ernest Hemingway's dog was no longer lying by his side as he typed his manuscripts, or chasing lizards by the pool, or resting his chin on the writer's foot when he read at night. "I miss Black Dog as much as I miss any friend I ever lost," he confessed. That the world keeps spinning in spite of this tremendous loss feels disorienting, even absurd.

For seven and a half
years we walked down
the calendar together,
step by step.

ETHEL SMYTH

As anyone knows who has lost
an animal companion, the
immediacy of the loss blows
through you as if you were an
abandoned farmhouse.

JACKSON GALAXY

I sat in the first floor room in which I work, watching my neighbors go about their lives, amazed and furious that they were behaving as if it was a normal day. Stop all the clocks. Buster was dead.

ROY HATTERSLEY

I once heard a woman who'd lost her dog say that she felt as though a color were suddenly missing from her world: the dog had introduced to her field of vision some previously unavailable hue, and without the dog, that color was gone. That seemed to capture the experience of loving a dog with eminent simplicity.

CAROLINE KNAPP

Marc Maron and Monkey at home,
Los Angeles, CA, 2020

# MARC MARON

The stand-up comic Marc Maron credits feral cats for helping him find his voice on air—first as a radio host and then as a legendary podcaster. In August of 2004, Maron discovered a litter of kittens in Astoria, Queens. He didn't know much about cats, but he figured out how to trap them in a shoebox and ferried them up to his apartment. Total chaos ensued. "They were just wild animals," he described years later. "I would go to sleep and I would hear them out there and I didn't know what they were doing, and I would wake up and my entire apartment was destroyed."

Maron was hosting a political radio show on Air America at the time, and told his listeners about the kitten crisis at home. They responded with advice and helpful cat tips, forecasting the loyal fellowship of his much broader audience today. In 2009, after the radio show was cancelled, he launched the early episodes of his podcast, *WTF*, then moved to Los Angeles with two of those feral cats, Monkey and LaFonda. Recovering from the end of his marriage and feeling hopeless, he poured his energy into *WTF*, which he recorded from his garage as a Hail Mary during a dark time.

The show changed the landscape of podcasting. Maron masterfully interviews celebrated personalities—comics, actors, musicians, writers, and other cultural icons, notably

President Obama, who took a motorcade to Maron's garage while still in office—and lets the conversations wander to unexpected places. The show opens with a monologue—he riffs about his personal life, the state of the world, and the health and antics of his cats.

LaFonda died in 2019, Monkey in 2020. Figuring out how to care for them had connected him to his listeners, and at the end of their lives, Maron shared his heartbreak with the same audience that those kittens had helped him build. "He knew I was sad," he said of his cat Monkey, "and I told him, I said, 'Look, I'm going to be okay.'"

I was the crying man leaving the vet's office with an empty carrier.

MARC MARON

Winkie is dead.
I can hardly bear to write
about it, but I had to let
you know.

P. G. WODEHOUSE

It was calamitous for me. I feel
a deep, deep grief. . . . I think of
Augustus. He was the sum of my
experiences. He had taken on my
outlook, my way of living.

V. S. NAIPAUL

Blemie's death was a blow. I knew I would miss him badly when he went, but I had no idea how badly.

EUGENE O'NEILL

I was not at all prepared for the volcanic eruption of woe when I left the vet's. I was crying so much I forgot to pay the bill and had to go back, and all the way home I could hardly see to drive. I felt cracked in two.

MAY SARTON

Alison Bechdel and Julia on their porch,
Duxbury, VT, 1993

# ALISON BECHDEL

Cartoonist Alison Bechdel started drawing as a kid and never stopped. "I spent the better part of my childhood holed up in makeshift offices that I would construct around the house, drawing under a high-intensity lamp." After college, she began to draw comics for *WomaNews*, a feminist monthly newspaper in New York City. For a young lesbian who didn't see herself represented in our culture, comics were a way to draw herself into the frame. Her strip, which she called *Dykes to Watch Out For*, ran for twenty-five years in over fifty alternative newspapers. By the time she was thirty, Bechdel had quit her day job to work as a full-time cartoonist.

The strip paved the way for Bechdel's pioneering graphic memoirs. In 2006 she published her first, *Fun Home*, a portrait of her childhood growing up in a small town in Pennsylvania; her relationship with her gay, closeted father; and her own coming out in college. The book, which pushes the boundaries of the graphic novel and memoir, received critical acclaim and put her on the literary map (and was later adapted into a Tony Award–winning Broadway musical).

Bechdel's tortoiseshell cat, Julia, was the ballast through it all: "She was just always there as I plodded away," she recalled. "On my lap, weighing down my arm as I was trying to type. Insinuating herself right onto my drawing board and threatening to smudge the fresh ink with her tail. Pulling up the masking tape that sticks my paper to the board with her teeth and trying to eat it. Demanding that I stop already and go out for a walk with her."

They were huddled together as she mapped out ideas for her next book project, her second graphic memoir, *Are You My Mother?* But Julia died just before the proposal was completed. In her absence, Bechdel wondered if her creativity might falter. "Or worse, what if I can't do it at all?" she worried. "I know, I know. I'll be okay. But I always felt like Julia was my muse—not in the sense that she inspired my work, but in the way that she literally oversaw it."

My beloved cat Julia, my constant companion, the small sun I've been orbiting for the past eighteen years, died on January 3rd.

———

ALISON BECHDEL

I have not been writing to you lately because Basket died and we ... just cried and cried and cried. We are a little better now but it is still pretty bad, and now we do not know quite what to do.

GERTRUDE STEIN

Never in my career had I suffered writer's block until we lost Trixie. I sat at the keyboard day after day, in the middle of *The Darkest Evening of the Year*, a story full of golden retrievers, and could not advance the manuscript by a single word.

DEAN KOONTZ

I placed an ad in
the papers: "Lost:
mongoose, answers
to the name of Kiria."
There was no reply.
None of the neighbors
had seen her.... She had
disappeared forever....
I was grief-stricken for
a long time.

---

PABLO NERUDA

It seems as if I could almost give my right hand to have thee back. A vital part of me is gone, something that knitted me to the fields and woods, and that made life more sweet.

———

JOHN BURROUGHS

I couldn't believe that she was gone, even though she'd been sick for so long. I could feel that something huge, a tide, had washed in, and then washed out.

———

ANNE LAMOTT

# BARACK OBAMA

On the unseasonably warm evening of November 4, 2008, a crowd of tens of thousands gathered in Grant Park in Chicago to watch the presidential election returns on giant screens. At 10 p.m. central time, CNN declared Obama the projected winner—the country's first African American president—a historic moment shared by the jubilant crowd that had by then grown to nearly a quarter million. "If there is anyone out there who still doubts that America is a place where all things are possible," he told the sea of ecstatic supporters stretched out before him, "who still wonders if the dream of our founders is alive in our time, who still questions the power of our democracy, tonight is your answer."

Before continuing with his victory speech, Obama thanked those who helped bring him to this moment, especially the love of his life—the future First Lady— and then he spoke to his daughters: "Sasha and Malia, I love you both more than you can imagine, and you have earned the new puppy that's coming with us to the White House!" Win or lose the election, the Obamas had promised their daughters a dog.

In the spring of 2009, the family introduced their new puppy to the world, a six-month-old Portuguese water dog, a gift from the late Senator Edward Kennedy.

"Of all the pleasures that first year in the White House would deliver," Obama wrote, "none quite compared to the mid-April arrival of Bo, a huggable, four-legged black bundle of fur, with a snowy-white chest and front paws."

In the summer of 2013, another puppy joined the family. "Early in Barack's second term, we'd added a new puppy to the household—Sunny—a free-spirited rambler," wrote Michelle Obama in her memoir. "The dogs added a lightness to everything. They were living, loafing proof that the White House was a home." This sense of normalcy was important to the Obamas as they raised their two young daughters at 1600 Pennsylvania Avenue and worked hard to balance parenthood with the pressures of political responsibilities.

Twelve years after they introduced Bo to the world, the Obamas celebrated his life and mourned his absence. "Bo was supposed to be a companion for the girls. We had no idea how much he would mean to all of us," shared the First Lady in a tribute. "This past year, with everyone back home during the pandemic, no one was happier than Bo. All his people were under one roof again—just like the day we got him."

*overleaf*: Barack Obama and Bo playing on
the White House lawn, Washington, DC, 2009

For more than a decade, Bo was a constant, gentle presence in our lives—happy to see us on our good days, our bad days, and every day in between. He tolerated all the fuss that came with being in the White House, had a big bark but no bite, loved to jump in the pool in the summer, was unflappable with children, lived for scraps around the dinner table, and had great hair. He was exactly what we needed and more than we ever expected. We will miss him dearly.

BARACK OBAMA

# A dear dog he was.

ELIZABETH BARRETT BROWNING

Saturday was a sad day for all of us and I know that all of Fala's friends will also be sad to know that he slept [*sic*] away, and the little dog's story has come to an end.

ELEANOR ROOSEVELT

You don't realize how much a dog's presence defines the contours of your home until, in its absence, the walls seem to relocate themselves. You don't realize how many of your unconscious gestures—a glance into a certain backyard corner, a moment of extra care on the stair landing—are calibrated to your dog's internal GPS.

MEGHAN DAUM

Fletch died today. The emptiness he leaves—the places where he used to be.

WILLIAM S. BURROUGHS

To miss someone is to also miss what is supposed to be the same when you wake up. I've lost two dogs to old age and one to illness, and each death left me with such grief I lay mute in bed for days, because I could not bear missing the humor of their habits: their running up and down the stairs barking at ghosts, or lying in a small circle of sun on the porch, or standing still in the garden wearing a pleased look as a breeze pushed the hair from their faces.

AMY TAN

Beatrix Potter and Xarifa, 1885

# BEATRIX POTTER

Beatrix Potter didn't have an easy time finding a publisher for *The Tale of Peter Rabbit*. Undeterred, she financed the printing of 250 copies of a private edition. The books went quickly and within a couple months, she reprinted 200 more. When she showed a copy of this black-and-white version to Frederick Warne & Co., one of the companies that had rejected the original manuscript, the publisher asked her to redraw the illustrations in color and then released the first commercial edition in 1902. It was an instant bestseller.

The characters that inhabit one of the most beloved children's books of all time were drawn from Potter's early memories. Her family spent several months each year in the countryside, first in Scotland and later in the north of England, and it was in these landscapes that she studied and sketched the natural world. She didn't have to roam far for inspiration. She and her younger brother, Bertram, cared for a variety of pets—rabbits, dogs, mice, lizards, frogs, bats, and more. The power of her storytelling was rooted in her own childlike imagination, which she nurtured throughout her life: "I have just made stories to please myself," she admitted, "because I never grew up!"

When she was a teenager, Potter started keeping a diary in code and continued for more than fifteen years.

The entries, written in tiny scribbles, remained indecipherable until 1958, when a Potter collector broke the cipher shorthand, swinging open the doors to the writer's inner world. In those private pages, she recorded which day she "played much with Peter Rabbit," as well as her worries about the health of her other bunny. On October 2, 1892: "Much concerned with the toothache and swollen face of Benjamin Bouncer, whose mouth is so small I cannot see in, but as far as I can feel there is no breakage." She noted the death of Judy, her lizard, on April 20, 1885: "I have had a great deal of pleasure from that little Creature." The following year, she mourned the death of her mouse Xarifa, who four decades later would show up as a character in her book *The Fairy Caravan*.

Potter inscribed a copy of that private edition of the now classic story with an homage to the animal who inspired it all: "In affectionate remembrance of poor old Peter Rabbit, who died on the 26th of January 1901 at the end of his 9th year . . . whatever the limitations of his intellect or outward shortcomings of his fur, and his ears and toes, his disposition was uniformly amiable and his temper unfailingly sweet. An affectionate companion and a quiet friend."

On Oct. 18th. [1886] occurred the death of *Poor Miss Mouse*, otherwise *Xarifa*. I was very much distressed, because she had been so sensible about taking medicine that I thought she would get through.... Poor little thing, I thought at one time she would last as long as myself. I believe she was a great age. Her nose and eyebrows were white, and towards the end of her life she was quite blind.... I think she was in many respects the sweetest little animal I ever knew.

———

BEATRIX POTTER

# Naps won't be the same.

RICKY GERVAIS

# He was my closest confidant. Rufus heard everything.

WINSTON CHURCHILL

Our sweet little Moppet died yesterday, so all we tried to do was of no avail. Now she is buried in a beautiful spot near our back door, to become part of the Maine she loved.

RACHEL CARSON

Today really is hard for me. My special friend . . . I got at seventeen (two weeks before I won my very first Grand Slam) left me today. She was sixteen years young and up until a few days ago was still sprinting. . . . With my dad by my side we were able to say a loving goodbye. She was with me from 1999 until today and I miss her so much.

SERENA WILLIAMS

Studio portrait of Edith Wharton with Mimi and Miza, Newport, RI, ca. 1890s

# EDITH WHARTON

When Edith Newbold Jones was three years old, she was given a puppy, a formative experience for the future novelist and short story writer. The moment she met that small white dog, "a new life began for me," she recalled years later. Foxy, as she named him, became a primary emotional relationship for young Edith. "How I cherished and yearned over and understood him! And how quickly he relegated all dolls and other inanimate toys to the region of my everlasting indifference!"

Edith was a lonely, sensitive child, and it was her love of Foxy—and of reading and writing—that saved her. By eleven, she had attempted to write her first novel. By sixteen, she had self-published her first volume of poetry. Her mother didn't approve of her writing endeavors, and was focused on finding her daughter a socially acceptable husband and respectable marriage. Edith did eventually get married, to a man twelve years her senior named Edward "Teddy" Wharton.

In 1902 the couple moved to a sprawling property they named The Mount, in the Berkshire Mountains of western Massachusetts. It was a dog's and writer's paradise: Jules, Toto, Mimi, Mitou, and Miza, among other canines in the Wharton home, roamed the land and lounged on pillows placed under the dining room table.

Edith spent her mornings in bed writing longhand, a pot of ink within reach, a small dog or two tucked by her side. In her bedroom on the third floor, she wrote *The House of Mirth* and *Ethan Frome*.

The couple sold the property in 1911, eventually divorcing, and Edith moved to France, where she fell in love with five Pekingese over the next two decades: Tootie, Choumai, Petite Tootie, Coonie, and Linky, the last of her beloved dogs. "We really communicated with each other—& no one had such wise things to say as Linky," she wrote. Linky provided the same reassurance and emotional connection that Foxy had offered Edith as a child. "I wish she could have outlasted me," she admitted, heartbroken, in a letter in April 1937. Four months later, Edith died, the close of an astounding literary career: she published over forty books in forty years and was the first woman to win a Pulitzer Prize—in 1921, for her novel *The Age of Innocence*.

If you walk the grounds of The Mount, you'll find a small pet cemetery set on a hill marked with miniature gravestones, where four of the Whartons' dogs rest. From the window of her bedroom, where she crafted classics of twentieth-century literature, Edith could look down on the small graveyard below.

Thank you so much for your kind & sympathetic letter about Toots. I really think that everyone who knew her grieves for her as if she were a real little person—& indeed was she not, & of the rarest kind?

EDITH WHARTON

It's tough to lose your shadow. Mine weighed sixty pounds, with a rounded nose and pointed ears that look like they had been inherited from Rin-Tin-Tin rather than Lassie. Though the patrician name of a purebred collie was scratched on a piece of paper somewhere, he responded simply to Fred. He was the dog I always wanted, and he was my friend.

THOMAS M. BOYD

# There's a parrot-size hole in my life.

IRENE PEPPERBERG

The oldest, our queen, saw her seventeenth birthday but suffered a terminal affliction that defied devotion. The gravitational pull of her imminent departure cast a spell on the household. . . . My daughter attended every atmospheric shift, the daily reality of her stoic deterioration. We awoke through the night to do her bidding. When she passed quietly in my daughter's lap we mourned deeply, as fully as for any human being.

———————

PATTI SMITH

Ordinarily the death of a cat means little to most men, a lot to fewer men, but to me, and that cat, it was exactly and no lie and sincerely like the death of my little brother—I loved Tyke with all my heart, he was my baby who as a kitten just slept in the palm of my hand with his little head hanging down, or just purring, for hours, just as long as I held him that way.

JACK KEROUAC

Studio portrait of Jane Goodall and Rusty,
Bournemouth, UK, 1954

# JANE GOODALL

When the British primatologist Jane Goodall turned one year old in 1935, her father bought her a stuffed chimpanzee called "Jubilee"—a toy that commemorated the first chimpanzee born at the London Zoo and King George V's silver jubilee, or quarter century on the throne. "People said it would give me nightmares, but he became my favorite toy," she recalled. "I took him everywhere. I still have him now, though he's in his eighties, and rather delicate, so he doesn't travel."

Goodall and her younger sister, Judith, spent much of their childhood exploring the beaches and cliffs of Bournemouth on the southern coast of England, and looking after all sorts of animals: cats and dogs, horses, turtles, guinea pigs, legless lizards, a hamster, a canary, and snails (which they identified by hand-painting their shells with numbers). But it was a hound named Rusty who would become her most influential mentor: "My memories of childhood are almost inseparable from memories of Rusty," she explained, "an endearing black mongrel dog with a white patch on his chest. He was my constant companion, and he taught me so much about the true nature of animals."

Rusty belonged to the owners of the San Remo Hotel, located next door to the Goodall home. He visited

Goodall daily and she treated him as her own. "Woken up by the barking of my black angel," she recorded in her diary on June 24, 1951, "and I went down to let him in. As he was so nice & early morningy, I took him for a little walk—after dressing of course. Then—oh, we went on the cliff and round about—and then he went home for his breakfast. I went home for mine."

Rusty was easygoing and up for anything, as long as it didn't compromise his dignity. "I would put him into pajamas, put a bandage round his head, and put him in bed," Goodall remembered. "He went all floppy. . . . There was just one thing: of course, he looked really funny, but if you laughed at him he hated it. He would immediately walk away, trailing garments, so we had to hide our laughter."

He was a bright student: he learned to play dead and hide-and-seek, and he jumped through hoops, climbed ladders, and mastered obstacle courses. While she was teaching him tricks, he was preparing Goodall for her future work in Tanzania. Rusty was the first to show her that animals have distinct personalities, minds, and emotions. "This gave me great strength in my convictions and work with chimpanzees," she recalled. "Rusty died before I went to Africa. I could not have gone had he been alive."

It wasn't reading books or working with chimps that convinced me animals could think and feel. It was my dog, Rusty. We spent every waking hour together. I can still remember clearly the day he died. I was about twenty. I was in London out to dinner with my boyfriend and I got the call. I tried to carry on normally but I burst out crying. I was utterly devastated. The deaths of some of the chimps I've worked with were very upsetting but it wasn't the same as Rusty. The chimps were their own selves, they were quite separate— Rusty was part of me.

JANE GOODALL

Daddy was my Tibet,
my Himalaya, my Gouda,
my Buddha, my source
of calmness.

CESAR MILLAN

That cat was my longest
and most successful
relationship. Sixteen
years. It's not all about
humans.

JEANETTE WINTERSON

I was just under fifty when this animal came into my hands, and the fifteen years she lived with me were the happiest of my life.

J. R. ACKERLEY

Forgive the silence; but the trip to Munich—as you know—was an ordeal, and to top it all my bulldog, my much beloved Bunky, died while we were there. I'd had him eight years, and loved [him] more than anything in the world. It was like losing one's child, and I wept till I could weep no more.

TRUMAN CAPOTE

Raymond Chandler and imperious Taki,
La Jolla, CA, ca. 1948

# RAYMOND CHANDLER

Raymond Chandler was a late bloomer. He started publishing mystery stories when he was forty-five, a year after getting fired from his job at an oil company. His first piece, "Blackmailers Don't Shoot," appeared in the December 1933 issue of the pulp magazine *Black Mask*. In *The Big Sleep*, the first of his seven novels—released in 1939—he introduced the now legendary private detective character Philip Marlowe.

The same year that Chandler lost his job at the oil company, he and his wife, Cissy, introduced a Persian kitten to their home. Chandler described her as "all fur with four legs peeping out from under it." They called her "Take"—Japanese for bamboo and pronounced in two syllables—but the name was easy to mispronounce, and they changed the spelling to "Taki." For nearly two decades, Taki occupied a prominent place in their lives, accompanying the couple as they restlessly moved from rental to rental in Los Angeles—the city he brought to life in his fiction—and then finally to their last residence, a home they purchased in La Jolla, California, in 1946.

Chandler was a gifted and prolific letter writer, and we learn from his correspondence that the fluffy black kitten grew into an opinionated diva. Regal and judgmental, she would sit just out of reach of guests and celebrate their departure by tearing through the house. For several hours each day, Chandler forced himself to sit at his desk, regardless of whether he felt like writing. Taki would rest on the pages he planned to revise, "sometimes leaning up against the typewriter and sometimes just quietly gazing out of the window from a corner of the desk, as much as to say, 'The stuff you're doing's a waste of my time, bud.'"

The Chandlers' strong-willed cat made sure she was the couple's only feline: "We have never been able to have another, because Taki wouldn't let us. We picked up a stray kitten in the desert once and tried to bring it into the house, but she got so mad she vomited."

In photographs of Chandler from the '30s and '40s, Taki is a steady presence: lounging on his desk, draped around his shoulder, cradled in his arms. He shared the news of her death in his letters: "Thanks for the letter and Christmas card," he wrote to the mystery-story critic James Sandoe. "I didn't send any this year. We were a bit broken up over the death of our black Persian cat. When I say a bit broken up I am being conventional. For us it was tragedy."

Our Christmas was not a particularly happy one, since we lost our black Persian cat that had been with us for almost twenty years, and was so much a part of our lives that even now we dread to come into the silent empty house after being out at night.

———

RAYMOND CHANDLER

My friends wrote as many elegies for him in different languages as ever were poured forth by Oxford or Cambridge on the death of a crowned head.

SIR WALTER SCOTT

I remember perhaps best a card from my friend Ingrid Newkirk. "Damn them for dying so young," she wrote, in her inimitable inverse-perverse way. After reading that I laughed—the first real laugh I had had since Polar Bear died.

CLEVELAND AMORY

## CHAPTER 4

# The Persistence of Mourning

The sorrow can linger. We have lost not only a loved one and true ally but also a connection to older versions of ourselves. Pets accompany us through emotional milestones—the stresses of moves and breakups, the joys of marriages and births. Some take on the role of protectors, keeping a close eye on us as well as their younger human or animal siblings, even helping us to raise them. They may have also walked by our side through the death of loved ones, which helps explain why mourning a pet might remind us of past losses, compound grief that can persist for some time.

British composer and suffragette Ethel Smyth confessed that remembering her sheepdog in the pages of her memoir helped remove "a few sharp thorns" from her heart, "a merciful service the pen sometimes performs for a writer." Sharing her memories with her readers allowed for something else, too: "I want to join hands with those who are traveling the same road, and make them feel that they are not alone in their sorrow."

Not the least hard thing to bear when they go from us, these quiet friends, is that they carry away with them so many years of our own lives.

JOHN GALSWORTHY

One reason for the persistence of mourning is the pet's ability to serve as a bridge to other people, a bridge that is ultimately severed at the death of the pet. Veterinarians have described the phenomenon of *double death*.

ALAN BECK & AARON KATCHER

In every loss are all past losses. I weep for Cinnamon, my cat, and the deaths that have gone before.

JEAN BURDEN

When you lose a dog, you not only lose the animal that has been your friend, you also lose a connection to the person you have been.

JENNIFER FINNEY BOYLAN

Ann Patchett and Rose, Nashville, TN, 2005

# ANN PATCHETT

Reading Ann Patchett's works of fiction and nonfiction feels like reading the words of a close friend, if that friend is a supremely gifted storyteller. The title of her sixth novel, *State of Wonder*, is an apt description of what it feels like to be in the company of her writing: long after reading the last sentence, you're left wondering what will become of the characters she has brought to life.

Patchett learned early on that words can change the way you think: after she read E. B. White's *Charlotte's Web* as a child, her stepfather gave her a pet pig and she stopped eating meat. As the co-owner of the Nashville independent bookstore Parnassus since 2011, she has been passing on the transformative power of reading to others. If you walk into Parnassus, her dog Sparky might greet you at the door.

But before Sparky, there was Rose. Patchett didn't set out to adopt a dog on the day she met a small white puppy near a local park, but that auspicious moment turned into a sixteen-year love affair. Patchett published her first appreciation of Rose in 1997, in their early, blissful days: "We've had Rose a year now, and there has never been a cold and rainy night when I've resented having to take her outside. I have never wished I didn't have a dog, while she sniffed at each individual blade of grass, even as my hands were freezing up around the leash." Rose accompanied her to dinner parties and on errands and vacations. Friends wondered whether this attachment might be a sublimated desire for children. Not at all, Patchett clarified; Rose simply fulfilled her long-standing desire for a dog, and they both lucked out.

As Rose aged, she lost her hearing and mobility. After she died in 2012, Patchett wrote a remembrance, the bookend to that first essay from Rose's puppyhood: "She was loyal and brave and as smart as a treeful of owls. By explaining her talents and legions of virtues, though, I would not be making my point, which is that the death of my dog hit me harder than the deaths of many people I have known, and this can't be explained away by saying how good she was. She was. But what I was feeling was something else entirely." To help ease her sorrow, Patchett's friend encouraged her to assemble a photo album of Rose's life. She would feel worse at first but then she would feel better, her friend promised. "I arranged the story of her life. What I hadn't imagined was that it was the story of my life as well."

When I was in the ditch, my friend Susan told me to find old pictures of Rose, pictures of when she was healthy and young.... If you flip through the pages you see us age together, always the two of us, Rose in my lap, Rose at my side, other people moving in and out of the frame over time while my hand forever rests on Rose.

ANN PATCHETT

The cat's death struck me as the end of an era.... The end of my safe college life, the last of my thirty-inch waist, my faltering relationship with my first real boyfriend. I cried for it all and spent the next several months wondering why so few songs were written about cats.

———

DAVID SEDARIS

An epoch in our lives was finished when Cleo (short for Cleopatra) died. Our relationship to the world was perceptibly altered. Nothing else can give us her exultant response to the common affairs of the day. Nothing can quite replace the happy good nature that was always greeting us when we came home or that was mischievously waking us up in the morning, hurrying us out of doors after breakfast, or innocently urging us to go to the country where we all wanted to be.

———

BROOKS ATKINSON

# I'm just eager to be around people so I don't miss my dog.

FIONA APPLE

Grief depletes the body. Be sure you stay hydrated and eat well. Try to sleep and get some exercise daily. Good, reliable friends are critical. Tell them you need them.

KALEEL SAKAKEENY

It is very unreal, and one wonders when one will get used to it.... But, of course, one can not easily get over seven years of intimacy.

SIGMUND FREUD

Weeks have passed. And the pain has not subsided. Every time I think about it, my heart starts racing and I feel like I just got stabbed in the chest. It's a jolt, still. Gracie's death.

OPRAH WINFREY

Amy Tan at home with Bubba,
New York City, 2005

# AMY TAN

Amy Tan launched her literary career in 1989 with the publication of her debut novel, *The Joy Luck Club*. It was a meteoric success—critically acclaimed and an instant bestseller that cleared the way for other Asian American voices. In 1993, the story's screen adaptation was the first major Hollywood film with an all Asian American cast. Tan has gone on to write other bestselling novels, works of nonfiction, and children's books.

If you follow Tan's dispatches on social media, then you've probably heard about the antics of her small dogs, and if you've attended her readings, you may have spotted them. She and her husband, Lou DeMattei, are enchanted by Yorkshire terriers and have adopted a series of Yorkies over the years: Bubba, Lilli, Bombo, and Bobo, as well as Tux, a six-pound Maltese and poodle mix rescued at the age of five and a half.

Light and portable, the dogs accompany Tan everywhere, including on book tours. At the end of long days of travel, book signings, press interviews, and not enough sleep, her dogs provide comfort and calm: "Once you are in your hotel room, a room that is unfamiliar each night, you are alone with all the particles of the day swirling in your head—alone, unless you have a dog! A dog is happy to listen to you and disperse the particles with his wagging tail."

Bubba was an easy traveler: "He's a 'whatever' kind of guy. He'll go along with anything and jump into any bag and go anywhere—to India, to the manicurist, to a boring conference, even a conference for manicurists in India."

Tan planted a crab apple tree in her garden to honor her canine and feline family members. "At the base of the trunk are smooth stones carved with their names," she explains. "I included a stone for my cat Sagwa as well, even though she died long before we had a garden. The tree looks like a small weeping willow and by early winter, the leaves will have fallen off. In the spring, when the leaves return, always all at once, I imagine the dogs running in the garden again. The cat watches. The return of those leaves is both sad and a comfort."

# Grief is remembering how you once filled his bowl and seeing the perpetually empty one.

AMY TAN

We collect absences. They become a sad place, a room in our heart, that we can visit when we can handle it. This absence is very present now. I'm living in it. I'm sad.

MARC MARON

All my life I have been surrounded by animals (my killer Chihuahua, Pepsi, is sleeping at my feet at the moment) and my garden contains the graves of a Rhodesian ridgeback, four beloved German shepherds, and two little monkeys—all badly missed.

ARTHUR C. CLARKE

They say if you're lucky you'll get one really great dog in your life. Other dogs may do their jobs in their own unique and perfectly wonderful ways, but there will always be that dog that no dog will replace, the dog that will make you cry even when it's been gone for more years than it could ever have lived.

MEGHAN DAUM

Shall we ever laugh
again? If I could
only see a dog that
I knew in the old
times! and could put
my arms around his
neck and tell him all,
everything, and
ease my heart.

MARK TWAIN

Life gets to be a series of dogs,
I thought, and I ticked off those
I could remember. Ghosts in
the house suddenly. Old dogs.
When I slept and woke again,
it was cold half-light and I was
almost sure I heard the dog's
toenails against the hall floor
and his single, discreet bark to go
outside. I won't live with a
lot more dogs, and I won't live
with another dog like him.

———

LOUDON WAINWRIGHT

John Steinbeck and Charley,
Sag Harbor, NY, 1961

# JOHN STEINBECK

On a bright September morning in 1960, the novelist John Steinbeck said goodbye to his wife, Elaine, and set off from his home in Sag Harbor, New York, on an epic road trip that he later documented in his bestselling book *Travels with Charley*. Fifty-eight years old and feeling disconnected from his country, Steinbeck was compelled to drive the open road, over ten thousand miles of it, in search of America. By then Steinbeck was a towering literary figure, having already published *Of Mice and Men* (1937), *The Grapes of Wrath* (1939), *Cannery Row* (1945), and *East of Eden* (1952), among other celebrated works of fiction and nonfiction.

To prepare for his trip, he had ordered a custom pickup truck with a camper top, a temporary home on wheels outfitted with the amenities he would need for his three-month excursion—double bed, stove, heater, toilet, refrigerator. Steinbeck didn't set off alone; he invited his elderly poodle, Charley, to join him.

Charley (formally known as "Charles le Chien") was a good-natured traveling companion. Born on the outskirts of Paris, he responded "quickly only to commands in French" and was a "born diplomat." On the trip, he served as their ambassador, putting strangers at ease and making it possible for Steinbeck to start conversations with just about anyone. Charley also provided security: although he was gentle, his bark kept them safe at night. Mornings with the poodle, though, weren't easy. "Over the years he has developed a number of innocent-appearing ways to get me up," Steinbeck explained. "He can shake himself and his collar loud enough to wake the dead. If that doesn't work he gets a sneezing fit. . . . He liked traveling so much he wanted to get started early, and early for Charley is the first tempering of darkness with the dawn."

It's easy to picture the two of them barreling down the roads of America together: "Charley is a tall dog," wrote Steinbeck. "As he sat in the seat beside me, his head was almost as tall as mine." They drove through thirty-four states, on highways and backcountry roads, to rediscover this "monster land." *Travels with Charley* was released in the summer of 1962, the year Steinbeck won the Nobel Prize in Literature.

His road trip with Charley remains an iconic travelogue, although researchers have since discovered that Steinbeck fictionalized certain details and conversations. Still, *Travels with Charley* is an extraordinary record of friendship. Two and a half years after they set off on their cross-country adventure and nine months after the book's release, Steinbeck was missing his copilot: "Charley dog died full of years but leaving a jagged hole nevertheless."

Charley is dead and only recently I don't hear him in the night.

JOHN STEINBECK

I once had a dog named Beau. He used to sleep in a corner of the bedroom. Some nights, though, he would sneak onto the bed and lie right in between Gloria and me.... He was up there because he wanted me to pat his head, so that's what I would do. Somehow, my touching his hair made him happier, and just the feeling of him laying against me helped me sleep better. After he died there were a lot of nights when I was certain that I could feel him get into bed beside me and I would reach out and pat his head.

JIMMY STEWART

# I see him
# all the time.

---

TRACEY EMIN

The terrible part of it is that people suggest to me that I get a new cat, that I invite this new cat into the home I shared with Augustus. As if this one should just be replaced so soon. It shows a lack of understanding.

V. S. NAIPAUL

Another cat? Perhaps. For love there is also a season; its seeds must be resown.

IRVING TOWNSEND

# I may live to be an old man, but I shall not live long enough to forget Reb.

JOHN BURROUGHS

I was sitting reading one afternoon by my pool, and Harry was nearby—say, five feet away—and I happened to look over at him; he was staring off into some middle distance, prone, front paws crossed, and he just . . . sighed. This sigh was not a reply; it was Harry sighing to himself over something. I miss him a great deal.

EDWARD ALBEE

## CHAPTER 5

# The Final Gift

"There is nothing crueler than the fact that human and animal lifespans are so out of synch," writes journalist and author Susan Orlean. That we typically live much longer than the pets we love is deeply unjust, but nineteenth-century Scottish novelist and poet Sir Walter Scott asked us to think about it this way: "If we suffer so much in losing a dog after an acquaintance of ten or twelve years, what would it be if they were to live double that time?"

It can feel like an act of betrayal to seek out another animal companion too soon, but there is no set timeline to heal or right way to honor the friendship. If we're lucky, we will love a procession of animals over our lifetime, which, of course, means accepting the painful reality that we will inevitably have to say goodbye to them as well. "Grief is the obverse of happiness," the legendary record producer Irving Townsend reminds us. "They are two sides of a single coin, and only the vulnerable know either."

Remember, that this will pass, and with time, you will form a new routine and new chapters of your lives will open.

———————

CESAR MILLAN

I love Ira with my whole heart, but I miss George every single day. Ira isn't a replacement. He is a new beginning. A new love. He doesn't make the hole that George left go away. But he does make it smaller. And knowing that George would have, without a doubt, loved him, makes me so happy. And very sad. So I guess the best "advice" I can give to those who have lost their furry/feathered/fluffy/ scaly friends . . . don't try to forget them. Remember them always and love like they knew you could.

———————

LINDSAY ROBERTS

Near this Spot
are deposited the Remains of one
who possessed Beauty without Vanity,
Strength without Insolence,
Courage without Ferocity,
and all the virtues of Man without his Vices.
This Praise, which would be unmeaning Flattery
if inscribed over human Ashes,
is but a just tribute to the Memory of
*BOATSWAIN*, a *DOG*,
who was born in *Newfoundland* May 1803
and died at *Newstead* Nov. 18th, 1808.

LORD BYRON

Helen Keller and Phiz, Boston, 1902

# HELEN KELLER

The presence of animals fortified Helen Keller's world from an early age. In 1882, when she was nineteen months old, she lost her sight and hearing after an unexplained illness. By eight, she was already feeling protected by the family dog: "Jumbo is very strong and faithful," she observed in a letter to a relative. "He will not let anything harm us at night." Much credit has been given to her dedicated teacher, Anne Sullivan Macy, a graduate of the Perkins School for the Blind, but Keller's canine friends also played powerful roles in her life. "The charming relations I have had with a long succession of dogs results from their happy spontaneity," she recalled years later. "Usually they are quick to discover that I cannot see or hear. Considerately they rise as I come near, so that I may not stumble."

By the time she was a student at Radcliffe College in Cambridge, Massachusetts, Keller's triumphs were widely recognized. She published her bestselling memoir *The Story of My Life* while still an undergraduate, and she was on her way to becoming a world-famous activist, educator, and social reformer. On campus, her devoted Boston bull terrier named Sir Thomas, nicknamed "Phiz," could be seen walking with her to class and lying quietly by her feet. This was before animals were formally trained as guides for the blind. Phiz wasn't always docile, though. Keller lovingly described him as "so affectionate that sometimes when he runs to meet us and jumps on me, he almost throws me down." She graduated cum laude in 1904, the first blind and deaf student to earn a college degree in the United States.

Keller could not see or hear animals, but she followed their movements and sensed their delights: "I have just touched my dog. He was rolling on the grass, with pleasure in every muscle and limb. I wanted to catch a picture of him in my fingers, and I touched him as lightly as I would cobwebs." When she was in her fifties, she published an essay describing what she would wish to see most if she regained her sight for just three days. Her list was long and detailed—objects in her home, colors of nature, the bustle and arts of New York City— but her teacher and friends, including her canine companions, were at the top: "I should like to look into the loyal, trusting eyes of my dogs," she wrote, "the grave, canny little Scottie, Darkie, and the stalwart, understanding Great Dane, Helga, whose warm, tender, and playful friendships are so comforting to me."

I grieved for him
a long time, and
resolved never to
have another dog.
But everybody knows
how, in the course of
time, the proverbial
other dog arrives.

HELEN KELLER

After a suitable period
of mourning, I went to
Lux's grave and asked her
permission to get another
dog. She said I could.

———————

MAGGI HAMBLING

There will come a time when your
sadness and anger have gone away....
After a while, you may even feel that
you want to have *another* pet.
You and the people you love can
talk about those feelings. You'll all
know when you're ready.

———————

FRED ROGERS

The new dog will not be a replacement. Buster was irreplaceable. His successor will be a dog in his own right. But he will be a reassertion of all that Buster stood for: the incalculable blessing of possessing a dog.

ROY HATTERSLEY

Georgia O'Keeffe with one of her chow chows,
Abiquiú, NM, 1962

# GEORGIA O'KEEFFE

American painter Georgia O'Keeffe emerged on the art scene in 1916, when photographer and gallery owner Alfred Stieglitz first exhibited her charcoal drawings at his Manhattan gallery, 291. She would go on to become the first female artist to be given a retrospective at the Museum of Modern Art in New York City. In 2014, when her painting *Jimson Weed/White Flower No. 1* sold at auction for $44.4 million, it was the highest price paid for an artwork made by a woman to date.

O'Keeffe and Stieglitz fell in love and became a legendary couple in the art world. They moved in together in New York City and married in 1924. But if Manhattan was Stieglitz's center of gravity, it was the Southwest that pulled at O'Keeffe. In 1929 she spent the summer in New Mexico, and in the years that followed she continued to break away from their crowded city life to spend months of quiet introspection in the high desert. In 1949, several years after Stieglitz died, O'Keeffe moved there permanently. She spent winter and spring in her 7,000-square-foot adobe house and studio in Abiquiú, and summer and fall in her second home surrounded by a 21,000-acre property known as Ghost Ranch.

O'Keeffe was devoted to enormous fluffy dogs—her "little people," as she called them—who kept her company as she lived and painted in this stark landscape. In 1952, a friend gifted her two chow chow puppies, Bo (or "Bobo") and Chia, the start of her lifelong affection for chows, known for their thick coat, independent spirit, and fierce devotion. She brought several more into her life over the decades, including Chia II, Bo II, Inca, and Jingo, among others.

Unfriendly to visitors but adoring of O'Keeffe, her dogs were protective of the artist. They slept in her room, accompanied her on long walks, and joined her on painting excursions. "When I go out to work as I do this time of year," she wrote to a friend in 1955, "Bo goes along and sleeps in the shade of the car after looking about to see if there are any rabbits, antelope—or anything alive of interest." Years later, in the evenings, Inca and Jingo curled up near her while she listened to Beethoven's piano sonatas in her studio.

Bo held a special place in O'Keeffe's mind and memory. She was still thinking about him near the end of her life, in her nineties. In a letter of gratitude to a friend, the photographer Todd Webb, she recalled the day Bo died. "We drove out into the White Hills, dug a hole under a small-sized cedar bush and put my beautiful dog into it and covered him with earth and many rocks," she wrote. "I like to think that probably he goes running and leaping through the White Hills alone in the night."

Bo, I must write you this morning as I cannot speak to you. When I look out on the yellow cliffs and the red hills, I often wonder if you are running and climbing about out there and will you come to me in a few moments full of this fine air.

---

GEORGIA O'KEEFFE

No stone stands over
where he lies. It is on
our hearts that his life
is engraved.

---

JOHN GALSWORTHY

We all say to one another,
"It never gets easier." Well, of
course not; I would hope not,
anyway. If it did, it would mean
that it wasn't the companion
that died, but something inside
us along the way.

---

JACKSON GALAXY

All dogs go to heaven,
I was told in the days
after George's death.
It seems more like they are
emissaries from there. That
means George's memory
is his final gift. It orients
me back to the question
we faced before our best
morning outings: What will
we do with the rest of
our walk before we must
finally walk home?

JOHN DICKERSON

Eugene O'Neill and Blemie, ca. 1930s

# EUGENE O'NEILL

Eugene Gladstone O'Neill, the first (and so far only) American playwright to win a Nobel Prize in Literature, is well known for writing some of the finest plays of the twentieth century. He also wrote one of the most heartfelt tributes to pet love and loss ever published.

O'Neill and his third wife, the actress Carlotta Monterey, were living in France when they welcomed a Dalmatian named Silverdine Emblem O'Neill into their lives—"Blemie" for short. They relocated to the United States in the early 1930s, and eventually settled on a 158-acre secluded hillside ranch in Northern California they called the Tao House. There O'Neill created some of his most celebrated works, including *The Iceman Cometh* and his most autobiographical play, *A Long Day's Journey into Night*, for which he won his fourth Pulitzer Prize several years after his death. Their marriage was turbulent, and Blemie must have brought a sense of equilibrium to their home. Carlotta remembered that when the three would relax by the fire, "Blemie would sit first by me and then by Gene, not to hurt anybody's feelings."

The couple considered Blemie their surrogate child and spared no expense to make him content and comfortable: he slept in a four-poster bed and bathed in his own bathtub, which required a separate septic tank. After Blemie died on December 17, 1940, they were inconsolable.

To comfort himself and his wife, the playwright drafted "The Last Will and Testament of an Extremely Distinguished Dog." The text, written in Blemie's voice, encouraged the couple to bring another dog (preferably a Dalmatian) into their lives, to whom Blemie generously bequethed his "collar and leash and my overcoat and raincoat, made to order in 1929 at Hermès in Paris." He didn't want his guardians to dwell on his absence. He wanted them to move on: "I ask my Master and Mistress to remember me always, but not to grieve for me too long."

One last word of farewell,
dear Master and Mistress.
Whenever you visit my grave,
say to yourselves with regret
but also with happiness in your
hearts at the remembrance of
my long happy life with you:
"Here lies one who loved us and
whom we loved." No matter
how deep my sleep I shall hear
you, and not all the power of
death can keep my spirit from
wagging a grateful tail.

———

EUGENE O'NEILL

We who choose
to surround ourselves
with lives even more
temporary than our
own, live within a
fragile circle, easily and
often breached. Unable
to accept its awful
gaps, we still would live
no other way.

IRVING TOWNSEND

## ACKNOWLEDGMENTS

---

Thank you, first, to the team at Simon & Schuster:
I am grateful to CEO and publisher Jonathan Karp and
editor-in-chief Priscilla Painton, who championed this
project from the start. My editor, Hana Park, has been a
wonderful collaborator: with her steady hand and sharp
eye, she helped me shape years of research into the book
I wanted to write. My gratitude to copyediting manager
Jessica Chin, associate design director Ruth Lee-Mui,
senior managing editor Amanda Mulholland, and senior
production editor Jamie Selzer.

I am indebted to Mia Johnson for creating such an
elegant, consoling, and pitch-perfect design. I am lucky
to work with Susan Raihofer, my talented and kind agent
at the David Black Agency, who somehow makes even
challenging parts of the bookmaking process a pleasure.

I wrote the proposal for this book on the back porch
of the home of my friends Rich Remsberg and Lisa
Nilsson in western Massachusetts. Years later, I reviewed
the copyedits on that same porch. I am thankful for their
kindness, and for sharing their lovely spot so generously;

it will always be my favorite office. A big thank you, also, to Nellie Perera for her steady support throughout; Kate Fitzpatrick and Tanya Heinrich for their thoughtful edits; Deb Aaronson for her expert eye; Russell Fernandez for his title suggestions; Phil Palladino for his warmth and enthusiasm; and John Thompson for all the conversations and for cheering me on in that final stretch.

I am grateful to my family for their love and encouragement: my sister, Rachel Bader; my brother-in-law, Leon Lazaroff; and my niece and nephew, Eleanor and Isaac. A special thank you to my mom, Beverly Bader, for her generosity and wise perspective. She read the earliest draft and responded with insightful feedback, always.

I was honored to spend my days with the tenderhearted letters, diary entries, memoirs, and other personal writings of the individuals included in this collection. This book is a tribute to their words and to the animals they loved so fiercely.

And my heartfelt appreciation to spunky Pearl, who has been by my side, and to dear, dignified Snowflake, who inspired it all.

# Sources

## INTRODUCTION

### 1 "jagged hole"
Late April 1963, letter to Otto Lindhardt, in *Steinbeck: A Life in Letters*, ed. Elaine Steinbeck and Robert Wallsten (New York: Penguin Books, 1989), 771.

### 2 "calamitous"
Isaac Chotiner, "V. S. Naipaul on the Arab Spring, Authors He Loathes, and the Books He Will Never Write," *New Republic*, December 7, 2012, https://newrepublic.com/article/110945/vs-naipaul-the-arab-spring-authors-he-loathes-and-the-books-he-will-never-write.

### 2 "volcanic eruption of woe"
November 13, 1974, journal entry, in May Sarton, *The House by the Sea: A Journal* (New York: W. W. Norton, 1977), 18.

### 2 "Carlo died"
Late January 1866, letter, in *Emily Dickinson: Selected Letters*, ed. Thomas Herbert Johnson (Cambridge, MA: Belknap Press of Harvard University Press, 1986), 191.

### 3 "Blemie's death"
January 30, 1941, letter, in *As Ever, Gene: The Letters of Eugene O'Neill to George Jean Nathan*, ed. Nancy L. Roberts and Arthur W. Roberts (Rutherford, NJ: Fairleigh Dickinson University Press, 1987), 209.

### 3 "We were a bit broken up"
January 10, 1951, letter to James Sandoe, in *Raymond Chandler Speaking*, ed. Dorothy Gardiner and Kathrine Sorley Walker (Berkeley: University of California Press, 1997), 184.

### 3 "The immediacy of the loss"
Jackson Galaxy, *Cat Daddy: What the World's Most Incorrigible Cat Taught Me About Life, Love, and Coming Clean* (New York: Jeremy P. Tarcher/Penguin, 2013), 274.

### 3 "I can still see"
E. B. White, "Dog Training," in *One Man's Meat* (New York: Harper & Row, 1982), 163.

### 3 "Affection without ambivalence"
Sigmund Freud, letter to Marie Bonaparte, quoted in the introduction by Gary Genosko, in Marie Bonaparte, *Topsy: The Story of a Golden-Haired Chow* (New Brunswick, NJ: Transaction Publishers, 1994), 13.

### 3 "No matter how awful"
John Dickerson, "Every Dog Is a Rescue Dog," *Atlantic*, September 9, 2021, https://www.theatlantic.com/family/archive/2021/09/john-dickerson-goodbye-my-familys-beloved-dog/620010/.

## CHAPTER 1:
## A CIRCLE AROUND US BOTH

### 7 "shaggy ally"
Early 1863, letter to Thomas Wentworth Higginson, in *The Letters of Emily Dickinson, 1845–1886*, ed. Mabel Loomis Todd (Boston: Little, Brown and Company, 1906), 309.

### 7 "I think they are companions"
Mary Oliver, quoted in Dana Jennings, "Scratching a Muse's Ears," *New York Times*, October 6, 2013, https://www.nytimes.com/2013/10/07/books/mary-olivers-dog-songs-finds-poetry-in-friends.html.

### 8 "I just got a dog"
"Sunday with Mister C.: An Audio-Documentary by Andy Warhol Starring Truman Capote," in *Truman Capote: Conversations*, ed. M. Thomas Inge (Jackson: University Press of Mississippi, 1987), 294.

### 9 "He & I are inseparable"
*The Brownings' Correspondence*, vol. 9, ed. Philip Kelley and Scott Lewis (Winfield, KS: Wedgestone Press, 1991), 157.

### 9 "The best kind of background"
Ross Simonini, "An Interview with Ottessa Moshfegh," *The Believer*, December 1, 2020, https://believermag.com/an-interview-with-ottessa-moshfegh/.

10 "I could not believe"
Sarah Miller, "The Bridge Dog," *New Yorker*,
November 15, 2020, https://www.newyorker.com
/culture/personal-history/the-bridge-dog.

10 "My dog has a number of acquaintances"
Donna Tartt, quoted in Katharine Viner, "A Talent
to Tantalize," *Guardian*, October 18, 2002, https://
www.theguardian.com/books/2002/oct/19
/fiction.features.

11 "As character he not only"
*The Memoirs of Ethel Smyth*, abridged ed.
(Middlesex, UK: Penguin Books, 1987), 348–49.

13 "one of the greatest gifts"
"The Gift of Your Honest Self," interview by Phil
Hoose, in *Fred Rogers: The Last Interview and Other
Conversations* (Brooklyn, NY: Melville House,
2021), 29–30.

14 "I had a dog"
Fred Rogers, "Death of a Gold Fish," *Mister Rogers'
Neighborhood*, episode #1101, March 23, 1970,
https://vimeo.com/153417661.

15 "When I was little"
Fred Rogers, foreword to *When a Pet Dies* (New
York: Putnam & Grosset, 1998), n.p.

16 "I didn't have any"
Haruki Murakami, "Abandoning a Cat," *New Yorker*,
September 30, 2019, https://www.newyorker.com
/magazine/2019/10/07/abandoning-a-cat.

17 "I can still see"
E. B. White, "Dog Training," in *One Man's Meat*
(New York: Harper & Row, 1982), 163.

17 "For companionship I kept pets"
Keith Richards, *Life* (New York: Little, Brown and
Company, 2010), 39.

18 "The walk is the basic unit"
John Dickerson, "Every Dog Is a Rescue Dog,"
*Atlantic*, September 9, 2021, https://www.the
atlantic.com/family/archive/2021/09/john
-dickerson-goodbye-my-familys-beloved-dog
/620010/.

19 "I walk every morning"
Billy Collins, interview by George Plimpton, "The
Art of Poetry No. 83," *Paris Review*, no. 159 (Fall
2001): https://www.theparisreview.org/interviews
/482/the-art-of-poetry-no-83-billy-collins.

19 "For the last four or five years"
William Styron, "Walking with Aquinnah," in
*My Generation: Collected Nonfiction*, ed. James L. W.
West III (New York: Random House, 2015), 579.

21 "This pussy of ours"
Patricia Barey and Therese Burson, *Julia's Cats:
Julia Child's Life in the Company of Cats* (New York:
Abrams Image, 2012), 29.

22 "A cat–any cat–is necessary"
Ibid., 84.

23 "'Mini' soon became"
Julia Child with Alex Prud'homme, *My Life in
France* (New York: Knopf, 2006), 36.

24 "This you'll call sentimental"
June 2, 1935, letter to Ethel Smyth, in *The Letters
of Virginia Woolf, 1932–1935*, vol. 5, ed. Nigel
Nicolson and Joanne Trautmann (New York:
Harvest, 1982), 396.

25 "My rabbit is a big part"
Amy Sedaris, *I Like You: Hospitality Under the
Influence* (New York: Warner Books, 2006), 179.

26 "At home where we live"
"Our Neighborhood," in *Louis Armstrong, in His
Own Words*, ed. Thomas Brothers (New York:
Oxford University Press, 1999), 178.

27 "I don't sing to Tamas"
February 2, 1976, journal entry, in May Sarton,
*The House by the Sea: A Journal* (New York: W. W.
Norton, 1977), 196–97.

27 "I love to house"
Elsie de Wolfe, *The House in Good Taste* (New York:
Century Co., 1913), 169.

29 "I didn't come here"
*Liberace: An Autobiography* (New York: Popular Library, 1976), 13.

29 "Too much of a good thing"
*Mae West on Sex, Health, and ESP* (London: W. H. Allen, 1975), 19.

29 "I have a lot of dogs"
*Liberace*, xii.

30 "They are allowed anywhere"
Ibid., 289.

30 "If somebody were to ask"
*The Wonderful Private World of Liberace* (Paducah, KY: Turner Publishing, 2003), 73.

30 "When I travel"
Ibid.

31 "I have one dog"
Ibid., 82.

32 "The dachshunds have been running"
Spring 1893, letter to Nikolai Leikin, in Donald Rayfield, *Anton Chekhov: A Life* (Evanston, IL: Northwestern University Press, 2000), 293.

33 "Our cat is growing"
September 23, 1948, letter to James Sandoe, in *Selected Letters of Raymond Chandler*, ed. Frank MacShane (New York: Columbia University Press, 1981), 128.

34 "It is amusing to see"
May 1, 1952, letter to Burroughs Mitchell, in *Zora Neale Hurston: A Life in Letters*, ed. Carla Kaplan (New York: Anchor, 2003), 685.

35 "I don't know whether I told you"
May 27, 1936, letter to Elizabeth Otis, in *Steinbeck: A Life in Letters*, ed. Elaine Steinbeck and Robert Wallsten (New York: Penguin Books, 1989), 124.

36 "arguably the longest story"
Robert Thompson, quoted in Sarah Boxer, "Charles M. Schulz, 'Peanuts' Creator, Dies at 77," *New York Times*, February 14, 2000, https://www.nytimes .com/2000/02/14/arts/charles-m-schulz-peanuts -creator-dies-at-77.html.

36 "A hunting dog that eats pins"
Charles Schulz, one-panel cartoon, in *Ripley's Believe It or Not*, February 22, 1937.

37 "Well, I am going home now"
Charles M. Schulz, *Around the World in 45 Years: Charlie Brown's Anniversary Celebration* (Kansas City, MO: Andrews and McMeel, 1994), 31.

37 "Please drive slowly"
Ibid., 32.

37 "He had been an unbelievable joy"
Ibid., 31.

37 "Sort of puts things"
Charles Schulz, *Peanuts*, July 16, 1993.

40 "Snoopy's not a real dog"
*Charles M. Schulz: Conversations*, ed. M. Thomas Inge (Jackson: University Press of Mississippi, 2000), 24.

41 "My dog and my mongoose"
Pablo Neruda, *The Complete Memoirs*, expanded ed., trans. Hardie St. Martin and Adrian Nathan West (New York: Farrar, Straus and Giroux, 2021), 111.

42 "I used to carry"
Interview by Ira Cohen, in *Conversations with Paul Bowles*, ed. Gena Dagel Caponi (Jackson: University Press of Mississippi, 1993), 13.

42 "There was one pigeon"
Margaret Cheney, *Tesla: Man Out of Time* (New York: Touchstone, 2001), 282–83.

43 "I tell my dog"
Mandy Patinkin (@mandypatinkin), Instagram, January 25, 2022, https://www.instagram.com/p /CZJ4o9VL2lw/.

43 "I've got two cats"
Jane Davis, "Jeanette Winterson in Conversation," *ReaderJaneDavis* (blog), April 15, 2015, https://

readerjanedavis.com/2015/04/15/jeanette
-winterson-in-conversation/.

45 "to lodge a few poems"
"Introduction to Robinson's *King Jasper*," in *The
Robert Frost Reader: Poetry and Prose*, ed. Edward
Connery Lathem and Lawrance Thompson (New
York: Henry Holt and Company, 2002), 392.

45 "I had to make things understood"
Bela Kornitzer, "At Home with Robert Frost,"
*Wisdom*, NBC, November 23, 1952.

45 "His virtues are all gentle"
November 2, 1941, letter to Willard E. Fraser, in
*The Selected Letters of Robert Frost*, ed. Lawrance
Thompson (New York: Holt, Rinehart and Winston,
1964), 495.

46 "one-man dog"
Erastus H. Hewitt, "Robert Frost of Brewster
Village," in *The Proceedings of the Cambridge
Historical Society*, vol. 40, 1964–66, https://history
cambridge.org/wp-content/uploads/2017/08
/Proceedings-Volume-40-1964-1966.pdf.

46 "When at last"
David McCord, "For One It Was Gillie . . . For
Another a Poem," *Boston Globe*, February 3, 1963, 31.

47 "I have a black dog"
November 2, 1941, letter to Willard E. Fraser, in
*The Selected Letters of Robert Frost*, 495.

48 "Whenever it is possible"
Helen Keller, *The Story of My Life* (Boston:
Houghton Mifflin, 1905), 125.

49 "I talk of all these things"
December 10, 1859, letter to Mrs. Bowles, in *The
Letters of Emily Dickinson, 1845–1886*, 192–93.

49 "When I sit down"
Doris Lessing, "The Old Age of El Magnifico," in *On
Cats* (London: Harper Perennial, 2008), 244–45.

50 "Pekes. How understanding"
December 25, 1950, letter to Denis Mackail,
in *Yours, Plum: The Letters of P. G. Wodehouse*,
ed. Frances Donaldson (New York: James H.
Heineman, 1990), 179.

51 "He was as solid"
Pam Houston, "He Trots the Air," *Outside*, May 13,
2019, https://www.outsideonline.com/2395158
/pam-houston-horse-death?curator=MediaREDEF.

53 "As long as he heard"
Donald Clarke, *Billie Holiday: Wishing on the Moon*
(Boston: Da Capo, 2002), 216.

53 "Excuse me"
Billie Holiday, quoted in Verena Dobnik, Associated
Press, "Photographer Chronicles Intimate
Moments with Jazz Greats," June 22, 2009.

53 "The thing I remember"
Clarke, *Billie Holiday*, 215.

56 "I knew Mister wouldn't recognize"
Billie Holiday, *Lady Sings the Blues: The 50th
Anniversary Edition* (New York: Harlem Moon/
Broadway Books, 2006), 164–65.

57 "Tulip never let me down"
J. R. Ackerley, *My Dog Tulip* (New York: New York
Review Books, 1999), 29.

58 "The dog and I have"
October 20, 1958, letter, in *Lovingly, Georgia: The
Complete Correspondence of Georgia O'Keeffe and
Anita Pollitzer*, ed. Clive Giboire (New York: Simon &
Schuster, 1990), 318.

58 "When it is bedtime"
Alice Walker, "Frida, the Perfect Familiar," in
*Anything We Love Can Be Saved: A Writer's Activism*
(New York: Random House, 1997), 133.

59 "Purring in his sleep"
William S. Burroughs, *The Cat Inside* (New York:
Viking, 1992), 61.

**60 "I really like it"**
Ursula K. Le Guin, "Chosen by a Cat," in *No Time to Spare: Thinking About What Matters* (Boston: Houghton Mifflin Harcourt, 2017), 31.

**61 "My relationship with my two"**
"Dispatches: Hoping and Doing," *WTF with Marc Maron*, February 11, 2019, http://www.wtfpod.com/dispatches/hoping-and-doing.

**61 "I can't imagine my life"**
Tracey Emin, "My Life in a Column," *Independent*, June 20, 2008.

**62 "What or who is the greatest"**
"Proust Questionnaire: Edward Gorey," *Vanity Fair*, October 1997, https://archive.vanityfair.com/article/1997/10/edward-gorey.

**62 "I'm not someone"**
Jan Hodenfield, "And 'G' Is for Gorey Who Here Tells His Story," *New York Post*, January 10, 1973, in *Ascending Peculiarity: Edward Gorey on Edward Gorey*, ed. Karen Wilkin (New York: Harcourt, 2001), 4.

**63 "Between four and five"**
James Merrill Filstrip, "The Cat Quotes by Edward Gorey," *Cats*, May 1978, in *Ascending Peculiarity*, 68.

**63 "Most people who have"**
Stephen Schiff, "Edward Gorey and the Tao of Nonsense," *New Yorker*, November 9, 1992, https://www.newyorker.com/magazine/1992/11/09/edward-gorey-and-the-tao-of-nonsense.

**66 "In looking for something"**
*Floating Worlds: The Letters of Edward Gorey and Peter F. Neumeyer*, ed. Peter F. Neumeyer (San Francisco: Pomegranate, 2011), 128.

**67 "My little old dog"**
Edith Wharton, "Lyrical Epigrams," *Yale Review* 9 (October 1919): 348.

**68 "Dogs have such"**
Alex Witchel, "At Home with: Caroline Knapp; Reinventing a Life with a Dog of Her Own," *New York Times*, June 25, 1998, https://www.nytimes.com/1998/06/25/garden/at-home-with-caroline-knapp-reinventing-a-life-with-a-dog-of-her-own.html.

**68 "My beloved Chihuahua"**
Arthur C. Clarke, Terry Jeeves, Larry Farsace, and Keith Stokes, "Dinosaur Tracks," *ScientiFiction: The First Fandom Report* 1 (Winter 2004): 4.

**69 "It is nearly dark"**
Irving Townsend, "The Fourth Cat," in *Separate Lifetimes* (St. Johnsville, NY: Flying Dog Press, 2005), 156.

CHAPTER 2:
THEIR TIME MUST COME

**71 "appreciate the time"**
Fiona Apple, Facebook, November 20, 2012.

**72 "He has filled the corners"**
April 5, 1949, letter to Thornton Wilder, in *Staying on Alone: Letters of Alice B. Toklas*, ed. Edward Burns (New York: Liveright, 1973), 149.

**73 "A dog lives only"**
John Burroughs, "Recalling Some Dogs," in *Old Dogs Remembered*, ed. Bud Johns (San Francisco: Synergistic Press, 1999), 76.

**74 "Oh dear, how old she is"**
*The Ackerley Letters*, ed. Neville Braybrooke (New York: Harcourt Brace Jovanovich, 1975), 191.

**74 "She's eleven"**
Susan Orlean, "The Glory and Heartbreak of the Old Dog," *Medium*, October 5, 2020, https://susanorlean.medium.com/the-glory-and-heartbreak-of-the-old-dog-f61774512970.

**75 "The greatest problem"**
Edward Albee, "Harry Sighing," in *Dogs We Love*, ed. Michael J. Rosen (New York: Artisan, 2008), 37.

**77 "I was a bride"**
"When Death Comes," in *Devotions: The Selected Poems of Mary Oliver* (New York: Penguin, 2020), 285.

**77 "She was a puppy"**
Mary Oliver, quoted in Dana Jennings, "Scratching a Muse's Ears," *New York Times*, October 6, 2013, https://www.nytimes.com/2013/10/07/books /mary-olivers-dog-songs-finds-poetry-in-friends .html.

**78 "They are a kind of poetry"**
Mary Oliver, "Dog Talk," in *Dog Songs* (New York: Penguin, 2013), 119.

**78 "deepest sting"**
Mary Oliver, "Bazougey," in *Dog Songs*, 41.

**78 "What would the world"**
Mary Oliver, "Dog Talk," in *Long Life: Essays and Other Writings* (Boston: Da Capo, 2004), 31.

**79 "It is exceedingly short"**
Ibid., 29–30.

**80 "Charley is well"**
September 1962, letter to Otto Lindhardt, in *Steinbeck: A Life in Letters*, ed. Elaine Steinbeck and Robert Wallsten (New York: Penguin Books, 1989), 771.

**80 "Having an old dog"**
Jon Pareles, "Laurie Anderson Is Telling Stories, Hers and Ours," *New York Times*, October 15, 2015, https://www.nytimes.com/2015/10/18/movies /laurie-anderson-is-telling-stories-hers-and-ours .html.

**81 "Tavi, my cocker spaniel"**
January 1956, diary entry, in *The Diary of Anaïs Nin, 1955–1966*, vol. 6, ed. Gunther Stuhlmann (New York: Harcourt Brace Jovanovich, 1977), 36.

**81 "He is not doing badly"**
Doris Lessing, "The Old Age of El Magnifico," in *On Cats* (London: Harper Perennial, 2008), 243.

**82 "Last week, watching Darcy"**
Verlyn Klinkenborg, "Darcy at Her Days' End," *New York Times*, December 18, 2009, https://www .nytimes.com/2009/12/19/opinion/19sat4.html.

**83 "When you have dogs"**
Dean Koontz, *A Big Little Life: A Memoir of a Joyful Dog Named Trixie* (New York: Bantam Books, 2011), 165.

**85 "I just saw"**
Naomi Rea, " 'Turner Was a Really Raunchy Man': Tracey Emin on Why Her Infamous *My Bed* Is Really like a J. M. W. Turner Painting," *Artnet News*, October 13, 2017, https://news.artnet.com /art-world/tracey-emin-bed-margate-1115603.

**85 "Docket is not just"**
Tracey Emin, My Life in a Column, *Independent*, September 17, 2011.

**86 "It's simply a notice"**
"Emin's Cat Posters Taken by Collectors," BBC News, March 28, 2002, http://news.bbc.co.uk/2 /hi/entertainment/1898461.stm.

**86 "My house is five floors"**
"In Bed With: Tracey Emin," *Harper's Bazaar*, June 13, 2013, https://www.harpersbazaar.com /culture/art-books-music/interviews/a984 /tracey-emin-daily-routine-0613/.

**87 "If I'm honest"**
Tracey Emin, "My Life in a Column," *Independent*, September 17, 2011.

**88 "Roany was stoicism"**
Pam Houston, "He Trots the Air," *Outside*, May 13, 2019, https://www.outsideonline.com/2395158 /pam-houston-horse-death?curator=MediaREDEF.

**89 "What is so touching"**
January 11, 1979, journal entry, in May Sarton, *Recovering: A Journal* (New York: W. W. Norton, 1980), 30.

**91 "She is my best friend"**
Fiona Apple, Facebook, November 20, 2012.

**91 "These are the choices"**
Ibid.

**94 "Many of us these days"**
Ibid.

**95 "I have always loved"**
Dolly Parton, *Songteller: My Life in Lyrics* (San Francisco: Chronicle Books, 2020), 127.

**95 "He is enjoying"**
December 25, 1949, letter to Mina Curtiss, in *Staying on Alone: Letters of Alice B. Toklas*, ed. Edward Burns (New York: Liveright, 1973), 184.

**96 "Anyone who has ever"**
Cleveland Amory, "L'Envoi," in *The Best Cat Ever* (New York: Little, Brown and Company, 1993), 237.

**97 "Do they know"**
John Galsworthy, "Memories," in *Old Dogs Remembered*, ed. Bud Johns (San Francisco: Synergistic Press, 1999), 56.

**97 "Once again a member"**
Irving Townsend, "The Fourth Cat," in *Separate Lifetimes* (St. Johnsville, NY: Flying Dog Press, 2005), 149.

**98 "Do you know that"**
Jay Leyda, *The Years and Hours of Emily Dickinson*, vol. 2 (New Haven, CT: Yale University Press, 1960), 21.

**99 "Staunch & faithful"**
June 30, 1908, letter to Charles Eliot Norton, in *The Letters of Edith Wharton*, ed. R. W. B. Lewis and Nancy Lewis (New York: Charles Scribner's Sons, 1988), 155.

**101 "disappointing novelty"**
"'Der Wald' at the Opera," *New York Times*, March 12, 1903.

**101 "utterly unfeminine"**
John Yohalem, "A Woman's Opera at the Met: Ethel Smyth's *Der Wald* in New York," *New York World*, The Metropolitan Opera Archives, http://archives .metoperafamily.org/imgs/DerWald.htm.

**101 "I want women to turn"**
Ethel Smyth, *What Happened Next* (London: Longmans, Green, 1940), 210.

**102 "a huge sprawling"**
*The Memoirs of Ethel Smyth*, abridged ed. (Middlesex, UK: Penguin Books, 1987), 138.

**102 "Half St. Bernard"**
Ibid.

**102 "The rich color"**
Ibid., 348.

**102 "While I have been writing"**
Ibid., 157.

**103 "He was sixteen years old"**
Ethel Smyth, *Streaks of Life* (London: Longmans, Green, 1921), 91.

**104 "Gizmo was a somber cat"**
Neil Steinberg, "The Cat That Broke Things," June 1, 2021, *Chicago Sun-Times*, https://chicago .suntimes.com/columnists/2021/6/1/22462337 /cats-saying-goodbye-pets-gizmo-steinberg.

**105 "My favorite monk"**
"Elizabeth Gilbert on What Dogs Teach Us," *The Isolation Journals with Suleika Jaouad*, February 27, 2022.

## CHAPTER 3:
## IT'S TOUGH TO LOSE YOUR SHADOW

**107 "It was one of the worst shocks"**
John Burroughs, "Recalling Some Dogs," in *Old Dogs Remembered*, ed. Bud Johns (San Francisco: Synergistic Press, 1999), 77.

**107 "a sorrow of details"**
Natalie Angier, "The Ambivalent Bond with a Ball of Fur," *New York Times*, October 2, 2007, https:// www.nytimes.com/2007/10/02/science/02angier .html.

107 "I miss Black Dog"
A. E. Hotchner, *Papa Hemingway: A Personal Memoir* (Boston: Da Capo, 2005), 243.

108 "For seven and a half years"
*The Memoirs of Ethel Smyth*, abridged ed. (Middlesex, UK: Penguin Books, 1987), 349.

108 "As anyone knows"
Jackson Galaxy, *Cat Daddy: What the World's Most Incorrigible Cat Taught Me About Life, Love, and Coming Clean* (New York: Jeremy P. Tarcher/ Penguin, 2013), 274.

109 "I sat in the first floor"
Roy Hattersley, "How I Miss My Beloved Dog Buster," *Daily Mail*, January 11, 2010, https:// www.dailymail.co.uk/news/article-1242173/Roy -Hattersley-How-I-miss-beloved-dog-Buster.html.

109 "I once heard a woman"
Caroline Knapp, *Pack of Two: The Intricate Bond Between People and Dogs* (New York: Delta, 1998), 6.

111 "They were just wild"
Introduction to interview with Jay Roach, episode 1080, *WTF with Marc Maron*, December 16, 2019.

112 "He knew I was sad"
Introduction to interview with Joe List, episode 1146, *WTF with Marc Maron*, August 6, 2020.

113 "I was the crying man"
Introduction "Dispatches: LaFonda," *WTF with Marc Maron*, December 16, 2019, wtfpod.com /dispatches/la-fonda.

114 "Winkie is dead"
November 28, 1938, letter to William Townend, in *Yours, Plum: The Letters of P. G. Wodehouse*, ed. Frances Donaldson (New York: James H. Heineman,1990), 175.

114 "It was calamitous"
Isaac Chotiner, "V. S. Naipaul on the Arab Spring, Authors He Loathes, and the Books He Will Never Write," *New Republic*, December 7, 2012, https:// newrepublic.com/article/110945/vs

-naipaul-the-arab-spring-authors-he-loathes-and -the-books-he-will-never-write.

115 "Blemie's death"
January 30, 1941, letter, in *As Ever, Gene: The Letters of Eugene O'Neill to George Jean Nathan*, ed. Nancy L. Roberts and Arthur W. Roberts (Teaneck, NJ: Fairleigh Dickinson University Press, 1987), 209.

115 "I was not at all"
November 13, 1974, journal entry, in May Sarton, *The House by the Sea: A Journal* (New York: W. W. Norton, 1977), 18.

117 "I spent the better part"
*The Indelible Alison Bechdel: Confessions, Comix, and Miscellaneous Dykes to Watch Out For* (Ithaca, NY: Firebrand Books, 1998), 13.

117 "She was just always"
Alison Bechdel, "Onward and Upward," dykesto watchoutfor.com, January 7, 2007, https://dykes towatchoutfor.com/onward-and-upward/.

118 "Or worse"
Ibid.

119 "My beloved cat Julia"
Alison Bechdel, "Julia, R.I.P.," dykestowatchoutfor .com, January 5, 2007, https://dykestowatchoutfor .com/julia-rip/.

120 "I have not been"
November 25, 1938 (postmarked), letter, in *The Letters of Gertrude Stein and Carl Van Vechten 1913–1946*, ed. Edward Burns (New York: Columbia University Press, 1986), 616.

121 "Never in my career"
Dean Koontz, *A Big Little Life: A Memoir of a Joyful Dog Named Trixie* (New York: Bantam Books, 2011), 263–64.

122 "I placed an ad"
Pablo Neruda, *The Complete Memoirs*, expanded ed., trans. Hardie St. Martin and Adrian Nathan West (New York: Farrar, Straus and Giroux, 2021), 132.

123 "It seems as if"
September 30, 1881, journal entry, in *The Life and Letters of John Burroughs*, ed. Clara Barrus (Boston: Houghton Mifflin, 1925), 228.

123 "I couldn't believe"
Anne Lamott, *Plan B: Further Thoughts on Faith* (New York: Penguin, 2006), 86.

124 "If there is anyone"
Barack Obama, victory speech, Grant Park, November 4, 2008, YouTube, https://www.youtube.com/watch?v=7wJ-2Zu_Iic.

124 "Sasha and Malia"
Ibid.

124 "Of all the pleasures"
Barack Obama, *A Promised Land* (New York: Crown, 2020), 373.

125 "Early in Barack's second"
Michelle Obama, *Becoming* (New York: Crown, 2018), 392.

125 "Bo was supposed"
Michelle Obama (@michelleobama), Instagram, May 8, 2021, https://www.instagram.com/p/COn3gFLLC5r/?hl=en.

128 "For more than"
Barack Obama, Twitter, May 8, 2021, https://twitter.com/BarackObama/status/1391106025269440516/photo/1.

129 "A dear dog"
Maureen Adams, *Shaggy Muses: The Dogs Who Inspired Virginia Woolf, Emily Dickinson, Elizabeth Barrett Browning, Edith Wharton, and Emily Brontë* (New York: Random House, 2009), 45.

129 "Saturday was a sad day"
"My Day, April 8, 1952," *The Eleanor Roosevelt Papers Digital Edition* (2017), https://www2.gwu.edu/~erpapers/myday/displaydoc.cfm?_y=1952&_f=md002190.

130 "You don't realize"
Meghan Daum, "The Gift of a Great Dog," *Los Angeles Times*, May 15, 2013, https://www.latimes.com/nation/la-oe-daum-rex-pets-death-20130516-column.html.

130 "Fletch died today"
July 9, 1997, journal entry, in *Last Words: The Final Journals of William S. Burroughs*, ed. James Grauerholz (New York: Grove Press, 2000), 235.

131 "To miss someone"
Amy Tan, *Where the Past Begins: A Writer's Memoir* (New York: Ecco, 2017), 352.

133 "I have just made"
Linda Lear, *Beatrix Potter: A Life in Nature* (New York: St. Martin's Griffin, 2008), 426.

134 "played much with Peter"
*The Journal of Beatrix Potter from 1881–1897*, trans. (from code writing) Leslie Linder (London: Penguin, 1989), 426.

134 "Much concerned with"
Ibid., 277.

134 "I have had a great deal"
Ibid., 82.

134 "In affectionate remembrance"
V&A, "Peter Rabbit: The Tale of 'The Tale,' " n.d., https://www.vam.ac.uk/articles/peter-rabbit-the-tale-of-the-tale.

135 "On Oct. 18th."
*The Journal of Beatrix Potter*, 202.

136 "Naps won't be"
Ricky Gervais (@rickygervais), Twitter, March 11, 2020, https://twitter.com/rickygervais/status/1237708498542223360?lang=en.

136 "He was my closest"
Piers Brendon, *Churchill's Menagerie: Winston Churchill and the Animal Kingdom* (New York: Pegasus, 2019), 220.

137 "Our sweet little Moppet"
Linda Lear, *Rachel Carson: Witness for Nature* (New York: Henry Holt, 1997), 457.

137 "Today really is hard"
Serena Williams (@serenawilliams), Instagram,
November 24, 2015, https://www.instagram
.com/p/-enG0fMTEo/?utm_source=ig_embed.

139 "a new life began"
Edith Wharton, *A Backward Glance* (New York:
Touchstone, 1998), 4.

139 "How I cherished"
Ibid.

140 "We really communicated"
May 16, 1937, letter to William R. Tyler, in *The Letters
of Edith Wharton*, ed. R. W. B. Lewis and Nancy Lewis
(New York: Charles Scribner's Sons, 1988), 606.

140 "I wish she could have"
April 17, 1937, letter to William R. Tyler, in
ibid., 606.

141 "Thank you so much"
December 1, 1894, letter, in *My Dear Governess:
The Letters of Edith Wharton to Anna Bahlmann*,
ed. Irene Goldman-Price (New Haven, CT: Yale
University Press, 2012), 140.

142 "It's tough to lose"
Thomas M. Boyd, "Fred, a Dog Gone but Not
Forgotten," in *Old Dogs Remembered*, ed. Bud Johns
(San Francisco: Synergistic Press, 1999), 168.

143 "There's a parrot-size"
Irene Pepperberg, quoted in Natalie Angier, "The
Ambivalent Bond with a Ball of Fur," *New York
Times*, October 2, 2007, https://www.nytimes
.com/2007/10/02/science/02angier.html.

144 "The oldest, our queen"
Patti Smith, *M Train* (New York: Vintage, 2016),
270.

145 "Ordinarily the death"
Jack Kerouac, *Big Sur* (New York: Warbler Classics,
2019), 35.

147 "People said it would"
Jack Watkins, "I Remember: Dr. Jane Goodall,"
*Reader's Digest*, February 12, 2019, https://www

.readersdigest.co.uk/culture/celebrities/i
-remember-dr-jane-goodall.

147 "My memories of childhood"
Jane Goodall with Phillip Berman, *Reason for Hope:
A Spiritual Journey* (New York: Warner Books,
1999), 9–10.

148 "Woken up by"
Dale Peterson, *Jane Goodall: The Woman Who
Redefined Man* (Boston: Houghton Mifflin, 2006), 43.

148 "I would put him"
"Jane Goodall's Dog Blog—Rusty," December 28,
2016, *Perfect Pets*, https://perfectpets.com.au
/best-pet-blog/post/jane-goodall-s-dog-blog-rusty.

148 "This gave me great"
Ibid.

149 "It wasn't reading books"
Jane Goodall, interview by Jane Graham, "The Mix:
Letter to My Younger Self," *Big Issue*, September 10,
2012.

150 "Daddy was my Tibet"
Cesar Millan, quoted in "'Dog Whisperer' Bounces
Back," *Portland Press Herald*, November 16, 2012,
https://www.pressherald.com/2012/11/16/dog
-whisperer-bounces-back_2012-11-16/.

150 "That cat was my longest"
Jeanette Winterson (@Wintersonworld), Twitter,
August 20, 2020, https://twitter.com/winterson
world/status/1296546636404011008.

151 "I was just under fifty"
J. R. Ackerley, *My Father and Myself* (New York:
New York Review Books, 1999), 281.

151 "Forgive the silence"
January 16, 1961, letter to Alvin and Marie Dewey,
in *Too Brief a Treat: The Letters of Truman Capote*,
ed. Gerald Clarke (New York: Vintage International,
2005), 308.

153 "all fur with four legs"
*The World of Raymond Chandler: In His Own Words*,
ed. Barry Day (New York: Vintage Books, 2015), 191.

154 "sometimes leaning up"
March 19, 1945, letter to Charles Morton, in ibid., 187.

154 "We have never"
August 9, 1948, letter to James Sandoe, in *Raymond Chandler Speaking*, ed. Dorothy Gardiner and Kathrine Sorley Walker (Berkeley: University of California Press, 1997), 178.

154 "Thanks for the letter"
January 10, 1951, letter, in ibid., 184.

155 "Our Christmas was not"
January 9, 1951, letter to Hamish Hamilton, in ibid., 183.

156 "My friends wrote"
February 25, 1811, letter to Lady Abercorn, in *Familiar Letters of Sir Walter Scott*, vol. 1 (Edinburgh: David Douglas, 1894), 210.

157 "I remember perhaps"
Cleveland Amory, "L'Envoi," in *The Best Cat Ever* (New York: Little, Brown and Company, 1993), 245–46.

CHAPTER 4: THE PERSISTENCE OF MOURNING

159 "a few sharp thorns"
*The Memoirs of Ethel Smyth*, abridged ed. (Middlesex, UK: Penguin Books, 1987), 347.

159 "I want to join hands"
Ibid.

160 "Not the least"
John Galsworthy, "Memories," in *Old Dogs Remembered*, ed. Bud Johns (San Francisco: Synergistic Press, 1999), 56.

160 "One reason for the persistence"
Alan Beck and Aaron Katcher, *Between Pets and People: The Importance of Animal Companionship* (West Lafayette, IN: Purdue University Press, 1996), 205.

161 "In every loss"
Jean Burden, "A Leavetaking," in *Angel Whiskers: Reflections on Loving and Losing a Feline Companion*, ed. Laurel E. Hunt (New York: Hyperion, 2001), 42.

161 "When you lose a dog"
Jennifer Finney Boylan, "Inside of a Dog," *New York Times*, December 27, 2017, https://www.nytimes.com/2017/12/27/opinion/rescue-animals-dogs-adopt.html.

163 "We've had Rose"
Ann Patchett, "This Dog's Life," *Vogue*, March 1997.

164 "She was loyal"
Ann Patchett, "Dog Without End," in *This Is the Story of a Happy Marriage* (New York: HarperCollins, 2013), 280.

164 "I arranged the story"
Ibid., 281.

165 "When I was in the ditch"
Ibid., 281–82.

166 "The cat's death"
David Sedaris, Act 1 in "In Dogs We Trust," *This American Life*, episode 154, https://www.thisamericanlife.org/154/transcript.

166 "An epoch in our lives"
Brooks Atkinson, "Cleo for Short," in *Old Dogs Remembered*, ed. Bud Johns (San Francisco: Synergistic Press, 1999), 34.

167 "I'm just eager"
Carrie Battan, "Fiona Apple," *Pitchfork*, October 7, 2013, https://pitchfork.com/features/update/9234-update-fiona-apple/.

168 "Grief depletes the body"
Kelli Bender, " 'Grief Is Grief': Why the Death of a Pet Can Feel Worse Than Losing a Human Loved One," *People*, July 26, 2019, https://people.com/pets/pet-grief-counseling/.

**169 "It is very unreal"**
January 14, 1937, diary entry, in *The Diary of Sigmund Freud, 1929–1939: A Record of the Final Decade*, trans. and ed. Michael Molnar (New York: Charles Scribner's Sons, 1992), 214.

**169 "Weeks have passed"**
Oprah Winfrey, "Oprah's Saving Gracie," *O, The Oprah Magazine*, August 2007, https://www.oprah.com/omagazine/oprahs-gracie-what-i-know-for-sure/all.

**171 "Once you are in your hotel room"**
Amy Tan, Powell's Q&A, November 6, 2013, *PowellsBooks.Blog*, https://www.powells.com/post/guests/powell%E2%80%99s-qa-amy-tan.

**172 "He's a 'whatever' kind of guy"**
Lisa Robinson, "Amy Tan and Bubba," *Urban Dog Magazine*, n.d., http://www.urbandogmagazine.com/archive_inner_dog.php?id=37.

**172 "At the base of the trunk"**
Amy Tan, *Where the Past Begins: A Writer's Memoir* (New York: Ecco, 2017), 352.

**173 "Grief is remembering"**
Amy Tan, "Perfect Companions," in Emily Scott Pottruck, *Tails of Devotion: A Look at the Bond Between People and Their Pets* (San Francisco: Tails of Devotion, 2005), v.

**174 "We collect absences"**
"Dispatches: I'm Living in It," *WTF with Marc Maron*, May 16, 2016, http://www.wtfpod.com/dispatches/im-living-in-it.

**174 "All my life"**
Arthur C. Clarke, foreword to Roger A. Caras, *A Perfect Harmony: The Intertwining Lives of Animals and Humans Throughout History* (West Lafayette, IN: Purdue University Press, 2002), 14.

**175 "They say if you're lucky"**
Meghan Daum, "The Gift of a Great Dog," *Los Angeles Times*, May 15, 2013, https://www.latimes.com/nation/la-oe-daum-rex-pets-death-20130516-column.html.

**176 "Shall we ever laugh"**
June 12, 1904, letter to W. D. Howells, in *Mark Twain's Letters*, vol. 2, ed. Albert Bigelow Paine (New York: Harper & Bros., 1917), 759.

**177 "Life gets to be"**
Loudon Wainwright, "Another Sort of Love Story," in *Old Dogs Remembered*, ed. Bud Johns (San Francisco: Synergistic Press, 1999), 43.

**179 "quickly only to commands"**
John Steinbeck, *Travels with Charley: In Search of America* (New York: Penguin, 1986), 9.

**179 "born diplomat"**
Ibid.

**180 "Over the years"**
Ibid., 24.

**180 "Charley is a tall dog"**
Ibid., 33.

**180 "monster land"**
Ibid., 6.

**180 "Charley dog"**
Late April 1963, letter to Otto Lindhardt, in *Steinbeck: A Life in Letters*, ed. Elaine Steinbeck and Robert Wallsten (New York: Penguin Books, 1989), 771.

**181 "Charley is dead"**
July 23, 1963, letter to Dr. E. S. Montgomery, in ibid., 772.

**182 "I once had a dog"**
Jimmy Stewart, quoted in Stanley Coren, *Why We Love the Dogs We Do: How to Find the Dog That Matches Your Personality* (New York: Free Press, 1998), 148.

**183 "I see him"**
Mark Westall, "Tracey Emin: Detail of Love," *FAD Magazine*, October 27, 2020, https://fadmagazine.com/2020/10/27/tracey-emin-detail-of-love/.

**184 "The terrible part"**
Isaac Chotiner, "V. S. Naipaul on the Arab Spring, Authors He Loathes, and the Books He Will Never Write," *New Republic*, December 7, 2012, https://newrepublic.com/article/110945/vs-naipaul-the-arab-spring-authors-he-loathes-and-the-books-he-will-never-write.

**184 "Another cat?"**
Irving Townsend, "The Fourth Cat," in *Separate Lifetimes* (St. Johnsville, NY: Flying Dog Press, 2005), 156.

**185 "I may live"**
John Burroughs, "Recalling Some Dogs," in *Old Dogs Remembered*, ed. Bud Johns (San Francisco: Synergistic, Press, 1999), 75.

**185 "I was sitting"**
Edward Albee, "Harry Sighing," in *Dogs We Love*, ed. Michael J. Rosen (New York: Artisan, 2008), 38.

**CHAPTER 5:**
**THE FINAL GIFT**

**187 "There is nothing crueler"**
Susan Orlean, "The Glory and Heartbreak of the Old Dog," *Medium*, October 5, 2020, https://susanorlean.medium.com/the-glory-and-heartbreak-of-the-old-dog-f61774512970.

**187 "If we suffer"**
Sir Walter Scott, April 24, 1822, letter to Maria Edgeworth, in *Letters of Literary Men*, new illustrated ed., ed. Frank Arthur Mumby (New York: George Routledge & Sons, 1911), 84.

**187 "Grief is the obverse"**
Irving Townsend, "The Fourth Cat," in *Separate Lifetimes* (St. Johnsville, NY: Flying Dog Press, 2005), 156.

**188 "Remember, that this will pass"**
"Mourning Your Dog," *Cesar's Way*, July 29, 2019, https://www.cesarsway.com/mourning-dog/.

**188 "I love Ira"**
Lindsay Roberts (@nana_george), Instagram, November 4, 2021, https://www.instagram.com/p/CV4JXQ9IyRa/.

**189 "Near this Spot"**
Lord Byron, inscription on the stone monument for Boatswain in Newstead Abbey, Nottinghamshire, UK.

**191 "Jumbo is very strong"**
Helen Keller, February 21, 1889, letter to Dr. Edward Everett Hale, in *The Story of My Life and Selected Letters*, ed. Stuart Miller (New York: Chartwell Books, 2016), 167.

**191 "The charming relations"**
Helen Keller, "Tribute to a Dog," introduction to Mildred Seybert and Lyla M. Olson, *Taffy and Tuffy* (New York: D. Appleton-Century, 1942), n.p.

**192 "so affectionate"**
Helen Keller, February 4, 1903, letter to Eva Halliday, in William Wade, *The Blind-Deaf* (Indianapolis, IN: Hecker Brothers, 1904), 45.

**192 "I have just touched"**
Helen Keller, "The Seeing Hand," in *The World I Live In* (New York: Century Company, 1910), 3.

**192 "I should like"**
Helen Keller, "Three Days to See," *Atlantic Monthly*, January 1933, https://www.afb.org/about-afb/history/helen-keller/books-essays-speeches/senses/three-days-see-published-atlantic.

**193 "I grieved for him"**
Helen Keller, in *Selected Writings*, ed. Kim E. Nielsen (New York: New York University Press, 2005), 132.

**194 "After a suitable period"**
Stuart Jeffries, " "There Are Plenty of Schlongs in Art"—Maggi Hambling Defends Her Nude Sculpture of Mary Wollstonecraft," *Guardian*, December 16, 2020, https://www.theguardian.com/artanddesign/2020/dec/16/plenty-schlongs-art-maggi-hambling-defends-nude-sculpture-of-mary-wollstonecraft.

**194 "There will come"**
Fred Rogers, foreword to *When a Pet Dies* (New York: Putnam & Grosset, 1998), n.p.

**195 "The new dog"**
Roy Hattersley, "How I Miss My Beloved Dog Buster," *Daily Mail*, January 11, 2010, https://www.dailymail.co.uk/news/article-1242173/Roy-Hattersley-How-I-miss-beloved-dog-Buster.html.

**197 "little people"**
Roxana Robinson, *Georgia O'Keeffe: A Life* (Hanover, NH: University Press of New England, 1999), 493.

**198 "When I go out"**
October 24, 1955, letter to Anita Pollitzer, in Nancy Hopkins Reily, *Georgia O'Keeffe: A Private Friendship*, vol. 2 (Santa Fe, NM: Sunstone Press, 2009), 313.

**198 "We drove out"**
November 20, 1981, letter to Todd Webb, in Jack Cowart and Juan Hamilton, *Georgia O'Keeffe: Art and Letters* (Boston: Bulfinch Press/Washington, DC: National Gallery of Art, 1987), 273.

**199 "Bo, I must write"**
Undated letter, Georgia O'Keeffe Writings and Other Papers, Yale Collection of American Literature, Beinecke Rare Book and Manuscript Library, New Haven, CT.

**200 "No stone stands"**
John Galsworthy, "Memories," in *Old Dogs Remembered*, ed. Bud Johns (San Francisco: Synergistic Press, 1999), 57.

**200 "We all say"**
Jackson Galaxy, *Cat Daddy: What the World's Most Incorrigible Cat Taught Me About Life, Love, and Coming Clean* (New York: Jeremy P. Tarcher/Penguin, 2013), 274.

**201 "All dogs go to heaven"**
John Dickerson, "Every Dog Is a Rescue Dog," *Atlantic*, September 9, 2021, https://www.theatlantic.com/family/archive/2021/09/john-dickerson-goodbye-my-familys-beloved-dog/620010/.

**203 "Blemie would sit"**
Carlotta Monterey O'Neill, in *Eugene O'Neill Remembered*, ed. Brenda Murphy and George Monteiro (Tuscaloosa: University of Alabama Press, 2017), 209.

**204 "collar and leash"**
"The Last Will and Testament of Silverdene Emblem O'Neill," in *The Unknown O'Neill: Unpublished or Unfamiliar Writings of Eugene O'Neill*, ed. Travis Bogard (New Haven, CT: Yale University Press, 1988), 434.

**204 "I ask my Master"**
Ibid., 433.

**205 "One last word of farewell"**
Ibid., 434.

**207 "We who choose"**
Irving Townsend, "The Once Again Prince," in *Separate Lifetimes* (St. Johnsville, NY: Flying Dog Press, 2005), 172.

# PHOTO CREDITS

My sincere thanks to the archives and photographers whose images appear throughout the pages of this book:

ii: Courtesy of the collection of Robert E. Jackson. v: The Museum of Fine Arts, Houston, Barbara Levine and Paige Ramey Collection, museum purchase funded by the Caroline Wiess Law Accessions Endowment Fund. 12: The Fred Rogers Center at Saint Vincent College, Latrobe, Pennsylvania. 20: Photograph by Paul Child. © Schlesinger Library, Harvard Radcliffe Institute. Image W603114. 28: Eddie Sanderson/Archive Photos via Getty Images. 38–39: Courtesy of the Charles M. Schulz Museum and Research Center, Santa Rosa, California. 44: © The Rosalie Thorne McKenna Foundation, courtesy Center for Creative Photography, The University of Arizona Foundation. Image courtesy of Dartmouth College Library. 54–55: William P. Gottlieb/Ira and Leonore S. Gershwin Fund Collection, Music Division, Library of Congress. 64–65: © Harry Benson. 76: © 2005 Rachel Giese Brown. 84: Courtesy of Harry Weller. 92–93: © Ellen Rehak. 100: © National Portrait Gallery, London. 110: © Marc Maron. 116: © Amey Radcliffe. 126–27: Courtesy of Barack Obama Presidential Library. 132: Courtesy of Princeton University Library. 138: Yale Collection of American Literature, Beinecke Rare Book & Manuscript Library, Yale University. 146: © The Jane Goodall Institute/Courtesy of the Goodall Family. 152: © John Engstead/mptvimages.com. 162: © John Dolan. 170: © Joe Tabacca. 178: © 1991 Hans Namuth Estate, courtesy Center for Creative Photography, University of Arizona. 190: Library of Congress. 196: © Todd Webb Archive. 202: Bettmann/Bettmann via Getty Images.

# INDEX

SARA BADER has worked as an acquisitions editor for Princeton Architectural Press and a senior editor for Phaidon. In addition to editing visual culture books, she has conceived and researched quotation collections for both publishers, including *The Designer Says, Art Is the Highest Form of Hope,* and *Every Day a Word Surprises Me.* In 2010 she launched Quotenik.com, a growing library of verified quotations.